EVERYTHING
~ *IN THE* ~
LARDER

EVERYTHING
~ *IN THE* ~
LARDER

Traditional British provisions and how to prepare them

DAVID MABEY

BBC BOOKS

Published by BBC Books,
a division of BBC Enterprises Limited,
Woodlands, 80 Wood Lane, London W12 0TT

First published 1990
© David Mabey 1990
ISBN 0 563 36024 0

Cover photograph by James Murphy

Set in Itek Goudy
by Ace Filmsetting Ltd, Frome, Somerset
Printed and bound in England by Richard Clay Ltd, St Ives plc
Cover printed by Richard Clay Ltd, St Ives plc

Contents

Acknowledgements 7

Introduction 9

Chapter One: *Bread and Baking* 11

Chapter Two: *Soft Cheeses* 24

Chapter Three: *Salted and Pickled Meat* 32

Chapter Four: *Sausages* 46

Chapter Five: *Cooked Meat Products* 59

Chapter Six: *Potting* 69

Chapter Seven: *Raised Pies and Pasties* 82

Chapter Eight: *Smoked Fish* 96

Chapter Nine: *Ketchups, Condiments and Dressings* 107

Chapter Ten: *Preserves* 121

Chapter Eleven: *Cider* 149

ACKNOWLEDGEMENTS

A great many people generously helped in providing information for this book. In particular I should like to thank Claire Marriage of Doves Farm Flour, Hungerford; Jackie Gear of the Henry Doubleday Research Association at Ryton Gardens near Coventry; Carole Evans of the Roebuck, Brimfield; Alison Johnson, formerly of Scarista House, Isle of Harris; Tim Reeson of Reeson's Fine Foods, Blythburgh, near South-wold; Clare Benson of Clare's Kitchen, Rendcomb, near Cirencester; Peter Dixon of White Moss House, Grasmere; Ivor and Susie Dunkerton of Dunkerton's Cider, Luntley, Hereford and Worcester; and the National Federation of Women's Institutes.

I am also grateful to the following for permission to quote material from their published books: Victor Gollancz Ltd for *Scarista Style* by Alison Johnson; Century Hutchinson Ltd for *The Miller Howe Cookbook* by John Tovey; Thames and Hudson for *Food in Antiquity* by D. and P. Brothwell; André Deutsch and Penguin Books for *The Cookery of England* by Elisabeth Ayrton.

Finally, special thanks for their unfailing support of this project to David Collison of Third Eye Productions; Peter Ridsdale-Scott, Editor, Independent Productions, BBC Manchester; and Suzanne Webber of BBC Books.

INTRODUCTION

Four centuries ago Francis Bacon had this to say about provisions: 'The preparation of meats and bread and drinks, that they may be rightly handled, and in order to this intention, is of exceedingly great moment; howsomever it may seem a mechanical thing and savouring of the kitchen and buttery, yet it is of more consequence than those fables of gold and precious stones and the like.'

Some people might think that making provisions is simply a benign distraction, a happy pastime, and there's no denying that is part of its attraction. The sheer fun of it, the sense of achievement and the actual business of 'making things' against the odds are irresistible. Anyone who has wrestled with yards of sausage skin that seems to have a life of its own will know what I mean! But there is a more serious purpose behind those hours spent bending over pans of hot jam or trying to control the movements of an unwieldy lump of hot-water pastry.

Most of our daily foods are now produced commercially and the processes and the ingredients involved are beyond our control. Yet in recent months a series of scares and scandals have shaken public confidence in the activities of the food industry: salmonella in eggs and broiler chickens, listeria derived from factory-made soft cheeses, pâtés and cook-chill foods, pesticide residues in apple juice and many more unpublicised incidents have transformed people's attitudes to what they eat. They are demanding answers, information and reassurances from the industry. Is our food really safe? And if not, why not?

Beyond the scaremongering and the political mud-slinging between pressure groups and the industry, there's an urgent need for real action.

Consumers voted with their collective purse and shopping basket on the subject of E numbers and additives, and as a result food manufacturers had to take notice. Some have made token gestures, removing preservatives from their products but leaving colourings untouched. Others have gone much further, and should be applauded for doing so. But now a new barrage of issues has surfaced: the potential dangers of a whole arsenal of pesticides that are sprayed unceasingly on to virtually all crops; the hormones, growth-promoters and antibiotics administered routinely to most livestock, and even the conditions under which most animals are reared. These questions need discussion and answers.

Making your own provisions is one way out of this dilemma. It allows you to take full control over your food, what it contains and how it is made. But remember that 'making your own' means using the very best ingredients you can lay your hands on. There is no point in producing cider in the traditional way if the apples you press have been sprayed with all manner of pesticides; it is hardly worth making additive-free sausages at home unless you start with organic or naturally reared meat. What you produce will be food of real quality, and you can experiment with many different techniques and flavours. Home-made provisions have that stamp of individuality. They are unique, all your own work.

Once you have made your provisions, they need to be stored. For years the best place was in the larder which, until quite recently, was the natural ally of the kitchen stove. Now houses are built without larders, in the belief that the refrigerator and the deep-freeze will do the job just as well. Refrigerators may be safe, if used properly, and they are very useful for some things. But they harden good pastry, ruin the character of virtually all kinds of cheese and draw the flavour from most cooked foods. Home-made provisions deserve a larder! As a storehouse of good things it can contain some of Britain's best foods: smoked fish, hundreds of unique farmhouse cheeses, our regional hams and dry-salted bacon, potted meat and fish preserved under a protective layer of clarified butter, brawns and glorious raised pies, not to mention the rich assortment of ketchups, relishes, sauces and condiments that are the supporting cast for many of our finest specialities.

Good wholesome food is part of our birthright, and the British larder should be one of our proudest possessions. Its contents deserve to be saved, not as museum pieces or as relics of some imaginary Arcadia, but as blueprints for the future. A process of renewal is at work in food enterprises across the land – and every pot of home-made jam, every hand-raised pie helps to safeguard the legacy of the larder.

CHAPTER ONE

BREAD AND BAKING

Bread has been the staff of life for thousands of years. The first loaves were made with anything that was availble, from acorns, peas and beans to barley, oats, rye and wheat. The raw material was not milled at all, but roughly crushed or pounded using something like a primitive pestle and mortar, before being mixed with water and cooked over an open fire. By the Iron Age there were basic rotary mills made from massive stones which had to be turned laboriously by hand. The Romans improved on this idea by harnessing the natural forces of water to power the millstones.

In time, water-powered mills were joined by windmills, and for centuries these devices were an essential feature of the landscape. The miller, too, had a vital role in the life of the community. He ground the farmer's cereal crops and supplied both bakers and private individuals. Brown or 'black' flour made from oats or barley was the standard subsistence for most ordinary families; only the rich could afford white wheaten bread. In the seventeenth century, when Thomas Fuller wrote 'They that have no other meat, Bread and butter are good to eat', it was commonly believed that white bread was more nutritious than brown.

The refinement of white flour went hand in hand with the development of mechanically powered roller mills during the nineteenth century. The wheat was matured, blended, then dry-cleaned and wet-cleaned by a series of complex operations. Mechanical rollers cracked open the wheat berries, and the starchy part of the grain was separated from the bran and the rest. It was then pulverised, graded through meshes, bleached, processed and packed into bags as 'white flour'. To make brown flour, millers simply re-added some bran and wheatgerm at a later stage. With only a few changes, this is still how most commercial millers work.

As cities grew, millers found a huge market for their flour in the new bread factories. Traditional bakers struggled against the competition, the price of white bread dropped and baking virtually disappeared as an essential domestic skill – the convenience of buying a loaf, rather than spending time making it yourself, was too tempting for most people. The commercial bakers had to find ways of improving their production methods to cope with demand. The breakthrough – as far as they were concerned – came in the 1960s, with the development of the Chorleywood Bread Process. Workers at the Flour Milling and Baking Research Association, in Chorleywood, Hertfordshire, devised a method of reducing the time needed for fermenting and proving the dough by using a system of high-speed agitations in special mixers. Several hours' working and waiting could be cut to a few minutes. As a result most baking plants can now operate on an awesome scale. Dough is mixed in batches of about 350 kg; about 2 hours later it is transformed into bread for the shops. Special oscillating blade cutters can slice 70 loaves a minute, and a computer-controlled plant is capable of producing as many as 6600 sliced, wrapped 800 g loaves every hour. It sounds like a triumph of technology over craft.

But the tide is turning. For all its relentless, clinical efficiency, commercial baking produces bread that is soft, spongy, salty and without character. Much of this has to do with the speed of the bread-making process. More and more people are now demanding old-style 'heavy' loaves made using the traditional long fermentation time, not for sentimental reasons, but because the bread looks and tastes better. There is also the ever-present concern about additives. Bakeries may advertise that they take nothing out of their bread, without saying much about the chemicals they add and how safe they are. Potassium bromate, the industry's favourite white bread 'improver' (used to help the dough to rise), was banned in most European countries some years ago; it was not outlawed by the British Government until November 1989. Other substances may soon follow.

Support for 'real', unadulterated bread is growing, and traditional bakers are finding a new lease of life. They deserve to be encouraged, not simply because they produce good, safe food, but because they are helping to preserve a deep-rooted regional tradition that has given us Staffordshire oatcakes and Wiltshire lardy cake, plum bread from Lincolnshire, stotties, Sally Lunns and Cornish splits.

GUIDELINES FOR BREAD AND BAKING

1 Flour

Most bread is made from wheat because it contains gluten – a protein that gives dough its elasticity and holds the structure together when it is expanding due to the action of yeast. Tradition has it that you can't make good bread from 'soft' English wheat: it doesn't have sufficient gluten. North American and Canadian wheat, on the other hand, is 'hard' and rich in the essential bread-making protein. Today's bread flours are often a mixture of both.

There are several rules for choosing flour for home baking. First, look for stone-ground varieties. Stone-grinding is a gentle low-temperature process: it preserves vitamins, minerals and natural oils. By contrast, commercial roller mills, spinning at up to 1000 revolutions per minute, create high temperatures which can destroy these essential nutrients.

If you are making white bread, look for unbleached plain flour. If you are making 'brown' bread, you will need 100 per cent wholemeal or at least 85 per cent extraction flour (i.e. flour containing 85 per cent of the whole grain).

If possible, make bread with organic flour. This contains no additives and is produced from grain grown to strict standards without the use of pesticides or artificial fertilisers. (It's ironic that bran, with all its healthy virtues, is actually the most heavily contaminated of all cereal products. It is a storehouse for pesticide residues.) Organic flour is becoming much more readily available in wholefood shops and supermarkets and you should be able to find a reputable brand very easily. Look for the following names: Doves Farm, Shipton Mill, Pimhill, Rushall and Marriages'. Quite a number of smaller millers also distribute locally.

The same rules apply to other more specialist flours, such as oats, barley and rye. Although I haven't specified 'organic' flour in all of the following recipes, it should be your first choice.

2 Yeast

Two kinds of yeast are generally available. Fresh yeast comes in compressed blocks and is now sold in most wholefood shops. You will need 2 oz (50 g) for 3 lb (1.5 kg) flour. Simply mash the yeast with 1 teaspoon (1 × 5 ml spoon) of sugar till it becomes runny. Add about 5 fl oz (150 ml) of the warm water required for the recipe and leave in a warm place until the mixture becomes frothy. It is now ready for use.

Granulated dried yeast is sold in small sachets or packets. Use 1 oz (25 g) for 3 lb (1.5 kg) flour. Sprinkle the required amount into about 5 fl oz (150 ml) warm water with 1 teaspoon (1 × 5 ml spoon) sugar. Stir well and leave in a warm place until it becomes frothy.

3 Kneading

The purpose of kneading is to force air into the dough. Work it through your fingers, punch it, pummel it, turn it over and over. This can be done in a bowl or on a floured board, whichever is easier. Depending on the dough, this can take anything from 5–15 minutes. You should aim for a smooth, springy consistency. Watch carefully, because the dough usually changes quite suddenly.

4 Rising

Once the dough has been kneaded, cover the bowl with a damp cloth and leave it in a warm place to rise. It needs to be left until it has roughly doubled in size. This may take anything from 2–12 hours, depending on the temperature and the time of year. A warm airy cupboard will produce fairly speedy results; otherwise, simply wrap up the bowl in a blanket and leave it in the kitchen overnight.

5 Shaping

Once the dough has risen, cut it into pieces and shape it into loaves. Either form the pieces into balls and put on to a floured baking tray or put the dough into well-greased baking tins: half fill the tins and press down the dough so that it doesn't crack when baked.

6 Proving

This 'second rising' can be done by putting the loaves in a warm airing cupboard or kitchen once again – anywhere, in fact, that is moderately warm rather than hot. Leave for about 45 minutes until the dough is soft and puffy to touch. As a rule it is better to underprove, rather than overprove.

7 Baking

It is important to pre-heat the oven to the correct temperature. Precise details and baking times vary from recipe to recipe and also depend on the size of the loaf you are baking. As a general rule, bread needs to go into a hot oven for about 30 minutes, then it should be turned around, and the heat reduced for the remainder of the baking time.

To test when the bread is baked through, simply tap the base with your knuckle: it should give out a hollow sound. Then remove from the oven and put on a wire rack to cool.

100 Per Cent Wholemeal Bread

Doves Farm is probably the best-known producer of organic flour in the UK, and its range of products is widely available in wholefood shops and supermarkets. The business is run by Claire and Michael Marriage who recommend their strong organic wholemeal flour for this loaf.

Makes 1 or 2 small loaves

1 teaspoon (1 × 5 ml spoon) honey or brown sugar
10 fl oz (300 ml) warm water
1 oz (25 g) fresh yeast
1 lb (450 g) organic wholemeal flour

1 teaspoon (1 × 5 ml spoon) sea salt
2 teaspoons (2 × 5 ml spoons) sunflower oil

Dissolve the honey or sugar in 3 fl oz (75 ml) of the warm water and stir in the yeast. Leave in a warm place for about 15 minutes until frothy. Mix together the flour and salt in a bowl, then add the yeast mixture, the oil and the rest of the water. Form into a dough and knead well. Cover with a clean cloth and leave in a draught-free place for about 1 hour or until the dough has doubled in size.

Turn out on to a floured surface and knead again. Shape the loaf and place in a large, well-oiled bread tin. Leave to rise a second time for about 25 minutes.

Meanwhile, pre-heat the oven to gas mark 8, 450°F (230°C). Bake the loaf in the oven for 35–40 minutes. Remove from the bread tin and allow to cool on a wire rack.

DORIS GRANT LOAF

The original Doris Grant recipe was devised to take the hard work out of bread-making. It is unusual because no kneading is required in the process. The wholefood chain Cranks popularised this style of baking, although it is by no means the only champion of this excellent loaf.

Jackie Gear of the Henry Doubleday Research Association based at Ryton Gardens (the National Centre for Organic Gardening), near Coventry, rates this as one of the best breads of all, and this is her version of the classic recipe.

Makes 2 medium loaves

3 lb (1.5 kg) organic wholemeal
   flour
1 tablespoon (1 × 15 ml spoon)
   sea salt
2 tablespoons (2 × 15 ml spoons)
   sunflower oil

1 oz (25 g) fresh yeast
1 tablespoon (1 × 15 ml spoon)
   raw cane sugar
1½–2 pints (900 ml–1.2 litres)
   water

Mix the flour and salt in a bowl and slowly add the sunflower oil. Blend the yeast and sugar in a cup or small bowl with about 5 fl oz (150 ml) of the warm water. Leave in a warm place for about 10 minutes or until the yeast becomes frothy.

Add the yeast to the flour mixture and gradually pour in the remainder of the water. Mix well with your hands. Divide the mixture into two halves and put each into a warmed, greased baking tin. Cover with a cloth and leave in a warm place for 20 minutes or until the dough has risen.

Pre-heat the oven to gas mark 6, 400°F (200°C). Bake the loaf in the oven for 35–40 minutes. Remove from the oven, leave to cool in the tin for a few minutes, turn out and allow the loaves to finish cooling on a wire rack.

OATMEAL BREAD/ROLLS

For twelve years Alison and Andrew Johnson ran Scarista House, a remote hotel in a miraculous landscape on the Isle of Harris overlooking the Atlantic. From here they waged a passionate campaign against processed food and factory farming and acquired a prestigious reputation for their cooking – especially the quality of their bread. The following recipe is adapted from Alison's book, *Scarista Style* (Gollancz, 1987).

Oats have had a lot of publicity in recent months, with many claims about their importance in a healthy diet. Whatever the truth, there's no doubting that oatmeal bread is both nutritious and delicious to eat.

Makes 2 large loaves or about 30 rolls

2 lb (1 kg) fine oatmeal	2 oz (50 g) fresh yeast
2 teaspoons (2 × 5 ml spoons) sea salt	1 teaspoon (1 × 5 ml spoon) brown sugar
1¼ pints (750 ml) warm water	8 oz (225 g) wholemeal flour

Mix the oatmeal and salt in a bowl with 1 pint (600 ml) of the warm water. Leave to stand in a warm place for 1 hour. Meanwhile, prepare the yeast: mix it with the sugar and stir in the remainder of the water; leave in a warm place until it is frothy.

Stir the yeast mixture into the oatmeal mixture and add the wholemeal flour. Combine thoroughly. The dough will be very sticky, so use only one hand for kneading at first. Add some extra flour if it is too intractable, but the dough should remain rather soft. Form into loaves or rolls and leave covered with a damp cloth. It takes a little longer to bulk than an all-wheat dough.

Pre-heat the oven to gas mark 8, 450°F (230°C). Put the risen dough on to greased baking trays and bake for 30–40 minutes if making loaves or 10–15 minutes if making rolls, until nicely browned. Take out of the oven and leave to cool on wire racks.

SODA BREAD

Ireland's famous bread is different because bicarbonate of soda (baking soda) acts as the leavening agent instead of yeast; the recipe also calls for buttermilk or sour milk and usually includes some oatmeal. The quantity of soda needs to be sufficient to raise the dough, but not enough to affect the overall flavour. And the actual kneading is important too: you should aim for a slack, heavy dough that will spread slightly on the baking tray.

Soda bread is eaten with everything from the grandest lobster to the humblest pickled pig's trotter and it goes perfectly with that most Irish of drinks – Guinness.

Makes 2 medium loaves

1 lb (450 g) 100% wholemeal
    flour
4 oz (100 g) plain white flour
2 oz (50 g) fine oatmeal
1 level teaspoon (1 × 5 ml
    spoon) bicarbonate of soda

1 level teaspoon (1 × 5 ml
    spoon) sea salt
10 fl oz (300 ml) slightly sour
    milk or buttermilk

Pre-heat the oven to gas mark 8, 450°F (230°C).

Put the flours and oatmeal in a bowl and mix well. Then add the bicarbonate of soda and salt and sift thoroughly through the mixture. Gradually add about two thirds of the milk, knead, then carefully pour in the remainder, working the dough until it is slack but not sloppy.

Divide into two, form each loaf into a round, flattish shape and mark the top with a deep cross, so that it will divide easily into four when it is baked. Put the loaves on to a greased baking tray and bake in the oven for 15 minutes. Then turn down the heat to gas mark 6, 400°F (200°C), and cook for a further 15 minutes or until the loaves are browned but not overbaked. Remove from the oven and leave to cool on a wire rack.

WALNUT BREAD

Flavoured breads are becoming increasingly popular – especially in restaurants. They can add a new dimension to formal meals – at the beginning or at the end (with cheese) – and are equally versatile at home.

Makes 2 medium loaves

1 lb (450 g) plain white flour	1 oz (25 g) fresh yeast
8 oz (225 g) wholemeal flour	15 fl oz (450 ml) warm milk
½ oz (15 g) sea salt	4 oz (100 g) butter or margarine
1 oz (25 g) sugar	4 oz (100 g) chopped walnuts

Mix the flours, salt and sugar in a bowl. Cream the yeast with a little of the milk and add to the dry mixture. Warm the butter or margarine and blend in, together with the rest of the milk. Knead well, adding a little extra water if necessary. Cover with a damp cloth and leave in a warm place for about 1½ hours or until the dough has doubled in size.

Knead again, add the chopped walnuts and mix well so that they are evenly distributed throughout the dough. Shape into two loaves, put into greased baking tins and leave to prove in a warm place for 45 minutes.

Heat the oven to gas mark 8, 450°F (230°C), and bake the loaves for 30 minutes. Reduce the heat to gas mark 5, 375°F (190°C), and cook for a further 10 minutes. Take out of the oven and cool on a wire rack.

ONION BREAD

An excellent savoury bread that goes perfectly with cheese and benefits greatly from light toasting. It can be made with white or wholemeal flour.

Makes 1 medium loaf

1 lb (450 g) plain white or wholemeal flour	½ oz (15 g) fresh yeast
1 teaspoon (1 × 5 ml spoon) sugar	6 fl oz (175 ml) lukewarm milk
1 teaspoon (1 × 5 ml spoon) sea salt	4 fl oz (120 ml) lukewarm water
	1 tablespoon (1 × 15 ml spoon) vegetable oil
	4 oz (100 g) onions, chopped

Sift the flour, sugar and salt in a bowl. Mix the fresh yeast with a little of the milk, add to the flour mixture, then stir in the remaining milk and the water. Knead the dough, cover with a damp cloth and leave in a warm place for 15 minutes. Knead again for about 5 minutes, then cover the dough once more with a cloth and leave in a warm place for 1–1½ hours.

Meanwhile, heat the vegetable oil in a frying pan and sauté the chopped onions until translucent. Add to the risen dough and knead well, so that the onion is thoroughly dispersed. Form the dough into a large ball and put on to a greased baking tray. Pre-heat the oven to gas mark 5, 375°F (190°C), and bake the loaf for about 40 minutes or until nicely browned. Remove from the oven and leave to cool on a wire rack.

OATCAKES

Lancashire, Yorkshire, Derbyshire and Staffordshire all have traditional recipes for oatcakes. These thin floppy breads are very different from the hard 'biscuits' baked in Scotland.

In most North Country kitchens there was a bakestone at the side of the fireplace which was used, first and foremost, for oatcakes. Baking sessions would take up the best part of a day and the thin cakes would be draped over flakes (wooden racks) suspended from beams over the fireplace. These days the baking is best done on a griddle or hotplate.

Makes about 36 oatcakes

8 oz (225 g) medium oatmeal	4 oz (100 g) lard
8 oz (225 g) plain white flour	water
1 teaspoon (1 × 5 ml spoon) sea salt	

Mix together the oatmeal, flour and salt. Chop the lard into little pieces and rub into the dry ingredients using your fingers. Add water, little by little, and mix until you have a firm paste. Roll out on a floured board sprinkled with oatmeal, then cut into oval shapes. (Alternatively divide the dough into small balls and roll out individually.)

Bake on a hot ungreased griddle until firm. The oatcakes are cooked and browned on one side only. Remove from the griddle and cool.

PITTA BREAD

Thanks largely to Greek restaurants and doner kebab take-aways, almost everyone in Britain knows about pitta bread. These flat oval loaves with a versatile pocket inside them are ideally suited to all kinds of food: they can be cut into strips and eaten with Middle Eastern dips such as hummus; they can be stuffed with meat, fish and vegetables of every description; and they can be eaten straight from the grill, moistened with thick virgin olive oil and spiced with black pepper.

Traditional pitta bread is made with white flour, although the recipe can be adapted for wholemeal.

Makes 6–10 loaves

½ oz (15 g) fresh yeast
1 teaspoon (1 × 5 ml spoon) sugar
10 fl oz (300 ml) warm water
1 lb (450 g) plain white flour

½ teaspoon (½ × 5 ml spoon) sea salt
1 tablespoon (1 × 15 ml spoon) sunflower oil (optional)

Dissolve the yeast and the sugar in about 2 fl oz (60 ml) of the warm water and leave in a warm place until the mixture is frothy.

Sift the flour and salt in a mixing bowl and pour in the yeast mixture. Knead well and add sufficient of the remaining water to make a firm dough. Knead vigorously for about 15 minutes or until the dough is elastic. (For a softer dough, put some oil at the bottom of the bowl and roll the ball of dough so that it is glazed all over.) Cover with a dampened cloth and leave in a warm place for at least 2 hours or until the dough has doubled in size.

Knead again, then divide the dough into 6–10 balls. Roll out on a floured board and flatten each loaf so that it is about ¼ inch (5 mm) thick. Dust with flour and lay the loaves on a cloth sprinkled with flour. Cover with another floured cloth and allow to rise in a warm place.

Pre-heat the oven to gas mark 9, 475°F (240°C). When it is hot, put in the greased baking trays and leave for 10 minutes. Slide the loaves on to the hot trays, splash with a little cold water to stop them browning and bake for 6–10 minutes. Remove from the oven and cool on wire racks. The bread should be soft and white, hardly browned, with a pocket inside.

BARA BRITH

This 'speckled bread' is made throughout Wales, and is the Welsh version of the fruit breads produced in many parts of Britain. Originally it was a way of brightening up bits of dough left over from baking sessions. Fresh currants or blackberries were used in some of the early recipes, although dried fruit and candied peel are standard ingredients these days.

Makes 2 medium loaves

12 oz (375 g) mixed dried fruit
  (such as currants and sultanas)
4 oz (100 g) candied peel
1 pint (600 ml) warm water
½ teaspoon (½ × 5 ml spoon)
  ground mixed spice
2 lb (1 kg) plain white flour

2 teaspoons (2 × 5 ml spoons)
  sea salt
6 oz (175 g) lard
1 oz (25 g) fresh yeast
8 oz (225 g) Demerara sugar
2 eggs
clear honey for glazing

Put the dried fruit and candied peel in the water with the mixed spice and leave to soak in a warm place for about 2 hours. Drain, saving the warm spiced water to mix with the dough.

Sift the flour and salt in a bowl and, using your fingertips, rub in the lard. Blend the yeast with the sugar and a little of the reserved spiced water. Add to the flour along with the eggs. Blend thoroughly, adding enough spiced water to give a firm, elastic dough. Knead well, cover with a damp cloth and put in a warm place for about 1 hour so that the dough can rise.

Knead again and add the drained fruit, making sure that it is well distributed. Shape the dough into two loaves and put into greased baking tins. Pre-heat the oven to gas mark 8, 450°F (230°C), and bake the loaves for 15 minutes. Reduce the heat to gas mark 5, 375°F (190°C), and bake for a further 45 minutes. Remove the loaves from the oven and take them out of their tins; spread the tops of the loaves lightly with clear honey to give a shiny glaze and leave to cool on a wire rack.

CRUMPETS

Essentially a crumpet is a round flat scone with holes in it. You should be able to buy traditional crumpet rings, which are 3½ inches (9 cm) wide and 1 inch (2.5 cm) deep, from most good kitchenware shops. The secret of successful crumpet-making is to get the consistency of the dough just right: it should be like a batter, but if it is too thick the characteristic holes will not form. So it is a good idea to test out one crumpet first before cooking the whole batch.

There are two schools of thought about eating crumpets. Some prefer to add sweetness in the form of jam and honey; others like the savoury approach – a sprinkling of salt or some meaty spread.

Makes about 10

1¼ lb (500 g) plain white flour	½ oz (15 g) fresh yeast
1 oz (25 g) sea salt	1 pint (600 ml) warm water

Sift the flour and salt together in a bowl. Cream the yeast with a little of the warm water, mix well and add to the flour. Then carefully stir in the remainder of the water. Cover with a cloth and keep in a warm place until the dough has risen.

Add a little extra water and adjust the consistency so that you have a thin workable batter. Leave for 5 minutes. Bake in well-greased crumpet rings on a hotplate or griddle, filling the rings half-way up with batter. Turn the crumpets when the mixture is dry on top and browned underneath. Then remove the rings. (Test a single crumpet first to check the consistency of the batter.) Leave the crumpets to cool on a wire rack.

CHAPTER TWO

SOFT CHEESES

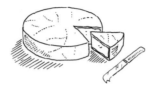

The first soft cheeses were probably made by accident. Nomadic tribesmen in parts of Eastern Europe and Asia found that milk left in the warm sun turned sour and formed a nutritious edible curd. Others may have noticed that milk carried in bags made from animals' stomachs gradually turned to cheese, thanks to the action of natural rennet present in the stomach bags themselves.

Almost all of these ancient cheese were soft. The idea of pressing and maturing curds so that they hardened came later. The production of hard and semi-hard cheeses required time, technical skills and equipment for pressing, as well as organised storehouses. Not surprisingly they developed on the farm, where there was a plentiful supply of milk and sufficient working space.

In Britain hard cheeses have reigned supreme for centuries. Cheshire makes claim to being the oldest, with records dating back to the eleventh century, but others such as Cheddar, Leicester and Double Gloucester still represent an enduring tradition. Added to this list are famous semi-hard cheeses, such as Caerphilly and Wensleydale, which are more lightly pressed and quicker to ripen than their hard-pressed neighbours.

While great Tudor households were building up storehouses packed with hundreds of monster hard cheeses, cooks in farmhouse kitchens were also producing small quantities of soft cheeses for quick consumption. These couldn't be stored for long and wouldn't travel without deteriorating, so they survived on their local reputation. By the beginning of the eighteenth century these soft cheeses were made only during the summer months as a special treat, while hard cheeses from almost every county in the land were for every-day eating unless, of course, you lived in Essex or Suffolk where the local speciality had an ominous reputation, vividly described in this anonymous rhyme: 'Knives won't cut me, fire won't sweat me; Dogs bark at me, but can't eat me.'

Best known was the so-called 'slipcote' cheese, named because of the ease with which its coat or rind would detach itself from the creamy ooziness within. Like other similar cheeses of its time, it was matured for about nine days between layers of nettles. Herb-flavoured cheeses were also popular, while others were delicately coloured with the juice of marigolds or spinach. Although most of these cheeses disappeared over the years, it was still possible to find some survivors in the 1930s. In *A Little Book of Cheese*, Osbert Burdett identified and eulogised about a dozen delights including Victoria, sweet and buttery and made at Guildford; Horner's from Redditch; and representatives from York and Cambridge. Today the best-known survivors are Colwick from Nottinghamshire and Scottish Crowdie. In the last ten years there has been a great revival in traditional cheese-making, and quite a number of new soft cheeses have been developed, often based on ewe's and goat's milk.

During the late 1980s, however, a shadow was cast over farmhouse cheese-making by listeriosis – a disease caused by *Listeria monocytogenes*, an organism that lives in the soil and can get into animal feed, particularly through badly stored silage and root feeds. Since 1983 there have been a number of cases of listeria, almost all of which have been traced back to pasteurised factory-made cheeses. And yet government action has centred on *unpasteurised* cheeses. As a result many small farmhouse dairies have been forced out of business and others have had to move over to pasteurised products, yet cheese-mongers are reporting an increase of interest in unpasteurised cheese since listeria hit the headlines. Apart from the fact that most experts think that cheese made from unpasteurised milk (with its quota of benevolent bacteria) is the best in flavour and quality, the crucial factors in producing good wholesome cheese free from harmful organisms are careful husbandry, hygienic milking and skilful cheese-making. Farmhouse cheese-makers generally take more care and their products can be trusted. The same principles apply if you are making soft cheese at home. Hygiene and care are the keywords for good safe cheese.

And when you are in the kitchen making soft cheeses, think also about their special qualities and remember Osbert Burdett's words: 'Theirs is the beauty of ephemeral things, and by this they are distinguished from their counterfeits. The refrigerator is a dangerous "friend" to them.'

GUIDELINES FOR MAKING SOFT CHEESES

1   First principles

Cheese-making depends on the unique characteristics of milk: its ability to clot and form a solid 'curd' and the fact that it can turn sour and become more acidic. It is a neat way of concentrating the solid nutritious part of the milk and removing most of the water and sugar.

The most common method of clotting or coagulating milk is to use rennet – a substance found in the stomachs of calves and other young mammals. It causes milk protein – casein – to form a solid, which makes it easier to digest. This process has been exploited by cheese-makers, who use rennet deliberately to form a curd which can be separated and pressed in different ways to produce all kinds of cheeses.

Rennet contains soluble calcium and is most effective when milk is warm. If the milk is boiled or heated to a high temperature – for example, in sterilisation or ultra-heat treatment (UHT) – the calcium becomes insoluble and the rennet will not work. Rennet is also active when milk is slightly sour. Certain bacteria can turn the natural milk sugar (lactose) into lactic acid, which gives the milk its sourness. Untreated raw milk contains these bacteria in abundance, but they are destroyed by pasteurisation – the heating process used to kill disease-causing organisms. Consequently, special bacterial cultures or 'starters' need to be used to begin the souring process.

Rennet curd is the basis of most hard and soft cheeses. Milk can also be made to clot simply by producing high acidity using a bacterial culture: this is the principle behind most acid-curd cheeses, yoghurts and other cultured-milk products. The curd is a concentrated storehouse of fat, protein and other nutrients, while the whey consists mostly of water and lactose. The aim is to separate curds and whey and develop the texture and flavour of the curd so that it produces a distinctive cheese.

2   Equipment

Very little special equipment is needed for making soft cheeses and much of it can be improvised from basic kitchen utensils.

A dairy thermometer, which floats on the surface of the liquid, is the best instrument for measuring temperature. A jam thermometer can be used in its place, although you will need to hold it in the liquid when testing. It is also useful to have an ordinary room thermometer to hand, so that you can check the temperature of your working area – whether you are incubating the starter, making the cheese or maturing it.

Squares of cloth are needed for draining the curd. These are best made from good-quality butter muslin (available from most fabric shops and hardware stores). Use pieces about 18 inches–2 feet (46–60 cm) square and make a double thickness. They need to be tied with string so that they can be hung up for draining.

Some soft cheeses can be made in moulds. In practice only French-style 'Coulommiers' hoops are readily available. These are in two parts, 4–5 inches (10–13 cm) in diameter and 5–6 inches (13–15 cm) high, with one hoop fitting inside the other. The top section is removed when the curd has sunk to the level of the bottom one. You can adapt square bottomless cake tins if you cannot obtain the proper moulds.

While the cheese is draining in a mould, you will need to put it on to some kind of wooden board. Find a piece of hard, well-seasoned wood about ½ inch (1 cm) thick.

In addition you will require an assortment of other basic kitchen items: a measuring jug, mixing bowls of various sizes, saucepans, a colander and spoons, ladles and knives. Always use stainless steel, plastic or wood where appropriate: never iron, zinc or aluminium as these will corrode.

All the equipment should be thoroughly cleaned or sterilised before and after each cheese-making session. Each item should be scrubbed or washed in boiling water, perhaps with some washing soda crystals or a proprietary brand of sterilising solution (available from chemists). Rinse in clean hot water before using.

3 Milk

Unless you live on a farm or have direct access to farm milk, you will need to make cheeses with pasteurised milk from your milkman or local shop. Sterilised and UHT milk are not suitable for cheese-making with rennet. Never use pasteurised milk that has 'gone off'.

As well as cow's milk, both ewe's and goat's milk can be used for cheese. If you want a low-fat variety, begin with skimmed or semi-skimmed milk.

4 Rennet

Rennet is an enzyme preparation made from the stomachs of calves and can be used to coagulate milk solids. Special cheese-making rennet is quite difficult to obtain and is generally used only for hard cheeses. But you can buy junket rennet from chemists and grocers and this is useful for making some soft cheeses, such as cottage cheese. It is available as a liquid or as tablets: use according to the directions on the packet. The disadvantage with junket rennet is that it produces rather bland results.

5 Starter

Cheese starter is essentially milk which contains a special bacterial culture, usually *Streptococcus lactis*, *S. cremoris* and *S. diacetylis*. These bacteria convert milk sugar into lactic acid, forming a curd and giving the resulting cheese some of its distinctive flavour. Packets of freeze-dried cheese starter are now available from many health food shops, or you can obtain them by mail order from R. J. Fullwood & Bland Ltd, Grange Road, Ellesmere, Shropshire SY12 9DF. One sachet will normally make about 2 pints (1.2 litres) of starter, but follow the instructions.

There are several stages involved in re-activating or re-cultivating the starter. Heat the recommended amount of milk to boiling point, then cool rapidly to 72°F (22°C) by standing the saucepan in cold water. Meanwhile, mix the contents of the sachet in a cleaned bowl or cup with a little water until you have a thin lump-free paste.

When the milk has cooled, stir in the paste and cover the pan. It must now be kept as near as possible to 72°F (22°C) for 12–24 hours. (In practice any temperature between 70°F and 80°F (21°C and 27°C) is satisfactory.) Put the pan near a radiator or stove or in an airing cupboard. (Some people use a clean warm vacuum flask, which keeps the milk at the required temperature.) The starter has done its work once the milk has thickened and begins to smell 'cheesy'.

You can then begin to make cheese (see pages 29–31). If you intend to make a second batch of cheese as well, save about 2 tablespoons (2 × 15 ml spoons) of re-activated starter and store in a sealed jar or bottle in the fridge until needed (it should keep for about a week). Alternatively you can divide the prepared starter into portions, freeze it and use each portion to inoculate the milk. A good way of doing this is to put about 2 tablespoons (2 × 15 ml spoons) of prepared starter into little polythene bottles (such as those in which lemonade or fruit juice is sold) which must first be thoroughly sterilised. Half-fill the bottles and freeze them lying on their sides. Before using the starter, allow it to thaw out naturally. Using this method you should be able to make 16 lb (7.25 kg) of cheese from one sachet of dried culture.

In time, the starter will gradually weaken and become less effective, especially if you use it regularly. If you notice dubious 'off' flavours and smells, you should buy a new batch of dried culture and begin again.

6 Flavourings

Soft cheeses can be flavoured with all manner of different ingredients: a little sea salt helps, but you can ring the changes with freshly chopped herbs, minced garlic, spring onions, nuts, fruit, olives – anything that takes your fancy. If you are using fresh ingredients for flavouring, the shelf-life and keeping qualities of the cheese will be reduced.

7 Storage

Most unmoulded soft cheeses can be packed in plastic tubs or containers with lids (thoroughly clean or sterilise them before use). They will keep perfectly well in a cool place, but are best eaten within 3 days (within 7 days if stored in a refrigerator).

Note: The following recipes are based on cow's milk. Other kinds of milk, such as goat's, may require lower renneting temperatures because they have smaller fat globules.

COTTAGE CHEESE

One of the best-known and most popular soft cheeses, cottage cheese, is usually made with skimmed or semi-skimmed milk with a low fat content. Before you begin, you will need to prepare some starter culture (see opposite).

Take 2 pints (1.2 litres) milk and heat in a double saucepan or over a bowl of simmering water until the temperature reaches 85°F (30°C): check with a thermometer. Then stir in 1 tablespoon (1 × 15 ml spoon) prepared starter. Dissolve 1 junket tablet or 2 teaspoons (2 × 5 ml spoons) liquid junket in a small amount of cold water and add to the milk immediately. Stir well and leave in a warm place for at least 2 hours or until the curd has set.

Once the curd has formed and while it is still in the saucepan, cut it up into roughly ½ inch (1 cm) squares with a knife. Then – very slowly – heat up the curds and whey until the temperature reaches 135°F (57°C). Stir carefully from time to time to separate the pieces of curd, but don't break them up too much, otherwise the final texture of the cheese will be ruined.

Meanwhile, set up a colander lined with a double thickness of muslin or cheese cloth. Stand the colander in a large bowl which will catch the whey as it drains. Once the correct temperature is reached, spoon the curds and whey into the muslin, leave in a warm place and allow to drain. (Alternatively you can tie the muslin into a bag, suspend it and collect the whey in a bowl.) Stir the curd from time to time until almost all the whey has drained out: this should take no more than 1 hour.

Once the cheese has drained properly, spoon out the curd, give it a final stir to produce the correct coarse mixture, then pack into a container. Add any other flavouring that you like at this stage (see page 29). Store in a cool place and eat within 3 days.

ACID-CURD (LACTIC) CHEESE

Curd cheeses, formed by the action of acid on milk protein, are very easy to make. Originally they were prepared from raw milk that had turned sour, but nowadays most people have to begin with fresh pasteurised milk and use a starter (see page 28) to create the souring.

Put 2 pints (1.2 litres) fresh milk (whole or skimmed) into a saucepan, bring to the boil, boil for 1 minute, then plunge the pan into a large container of cold water and leave until the temperature of the milk drops to 75°F (24°C). Transfer to a clean bowl and add 2 tablespoons (2 × 15 ml spoons) prepared starter. Stir well, cover and leave in a warm place at 70–80°F (21–27°C) for about 12 hours or until the curd has formed.

Set up a colander and muslin as described for Cottage Cheese (see above) and spoon in the curds and whey. At this stage you can add, say, 1 teaspoon (1 × 5 ml spoon) sea salt to taste. Scrape down the curd from time to time and stir to speed up draining. If the cloth becomes stiff or coated, you may need to change it. After about 2 hours the whey should have drained away and the cheese can be spooned out and packed into a suitable container. Store it in a cool place and eat within 3 days.

CREAM CHEESE

As its name suggests, this cheese is made from cream rather than milk. You can begin with either single cream – which needs rennet for coagulation – or double cream, which will drain without rennet but is improved with the addition of a starter. The butterfat content of each type may affect your decision: single cream is 18–25 per cent fat; double cream is 48–55 per cent fat.

Cream cheeses are traditionally moulded into small cylinders, rectangles or squares of various sizes. If no suitable moulds are available, you can improvise.

If you are using single cream, heat 1 pint (600 ml) to 75°F (24°C) and add ½ teaspoon (½ × 5 ml spoon) prepared starter (see page 28). Mix well, cover the bowl and leave in a warm place for 2–3 hours so that the cream can ripen. Then dilute ¼ teaspoon (¼ × 5 ml spoon) liquid rennet with six times its own volume of cold boiled water and add to the cream. Cover again and leave in a warm place at 70–80°F (21–27°C) for 8–12 hours or until the cream coagulates.

Spoon the mixture into a double thickness of muslin or cheese cloth, tie to form a bag and hang up in a cool place at 50–55°F (10–13°C) to drain; put a bowl underneath to collect the whey. Scrape the curd from the sides of the cloth from time to time, and change the cloth if it becomes clogged.

When the curd is completely drained, it should be thick and granular. Add 1 teaspoon (1 × 5 ml spoon) sea salt, mix well and pack into a suitable mould. Alternatively, shape into a round, square or rectangular pat and wrap in greaseproof paper. Store in a cool place and eat within 2–3 days.

Double-cream cheese is made in a similar fashion following the recipe above, but you do not need to add rennet. Also it is recommended that you include 2 teaspoons (2 × 5 ml spoons) sea salt with the starter to improve the drainage and keeping quality of the cheese.

CHAPTER THREE

SALTED AND PICKLED MEAT

During the Neolithic age . . . there was a systematic and deliberate exploitation of salt deposits. Salt eating may have started as a whim, the taste being naturally satisfying. In the train of this prehistoric 'consumer demand' for the luxury salt would follow the discovery that the mineral was of value in preserving other foodstuffs, especially animal tissues.

(From *Food in Antiquity* by D. & O. Brothwell,
Thames & Hudson, 1969)

Brine springs, rivers and lakes were exploited first by the Greeks and later by the Romans. Wherever there was salt it was mined or collected from surface deposits or from underground. And it was used almost exclusively for preserving meat, fish and animal hides.

By the Middle Ages salting and pickling meat dominated much of the kitchen work in English households. Livestock – cattle in particular – couldn't be kept alive through the lean winter months when there was little or nothing for them to eat. They therefore had to be killed in the autumn and their meat preserved by salting, to provide a supply of food until fresh meat was available again in early summer. Cattle were important, but the pig reigned supreme. It was the great all-purpose food animal of its day, a living larder, tended and nurtured until the time arrived for the killing, which was invested with much ritual and celebration. Above all, the pig provided bacon and hams, both of which were cured by dry-salting often backed up by smoking.

An essential part of pig killing and curing was 'souse', part of Christmas fare for the sixteenth-century Essex farmer Thomas Tusser, who recorded the year's work in a series of doggerel verses, *Five Hundred Points of Husbandry*:

> Good bread and good drinke, a good fier in the hall;
> Brawn, pudding and souse, and good mustard withal.

Once the animal had been cut up and the sides and hind legs were being salted for supplies of bacon through the winter, all the other parts – trotters, ears, tails, cheeks and so on – were put into a tub of brine and pickled. Collectively these items were known as 'souse'. They were often left right through the autumn and winter months, pieces being lifted out and cooked when needed. Although brine was the usual 'sousing drink', well-off households also made use of verjuice (from sour crabapples), wine or ale mixed with herbs and spices.

But there were many other kinds of salted and pickled meat, from beef to chickens and ducks. Both methods of preserving were popular, although meat was usually immersed in tubs of brine during the summer months to keep it out of the reach of flies and to stop it spoiling in the heat. In the winter it could be dry-salted without fear that it would putrefy or turn rancid before it was sufficiently cured.

Pickled meat was an important larder food both on land and at sea. From Elizabethan times onwards sailors relied on 'barrelled' pork, which they ate with dried pulses and rough ship's biscuits. This was very basic nourishment, so it isn't surprising that seamen devised a few curious recipes for broths and soups to brighten up the ingredients, making them marginally more palatable. Such stuff was still being produced and eaten well into the nineteenth century, although it wasn't liked by everyone. William Cobbett, a great believer in dry-salting, rather than 'wet pickling', called it 'sea junk' and thought there was 'nothing more villainous'.

As refrigeration and other methods of keeping and preserving food appeared in the wake of the Industrial Revolution, pickling and salting lost much of their importance as essential features of the food economy, although the production of bacon and hams has continued to flourish. Curing methods have become milder – the products are less salty, the meat less fatty. And it's ironic that bacon is now considered a perishable food – a world away from the winter provisions of the English farmhouse.

Producing bacon and hams may be impractical for most households, but small-scale pickling and salting are well worth trying. Today's farming methods, intensive rearing and new breeds, plus less care in hanging and butchery have taken their toll on much of our fresh meat. But a few hours in the pickling brine can give it a new lease of life. As Jane Grigson once said, 'Salting rescues the Sunday lunch.'

GUIDELINES FOR SALTING AND PICKLING MEAT

1 Ingredients

Always use very fresh meat, never frozen. If possible, try to obtain a supply of organic or naturally reared meat, which not only has a better flavour but will also be free of growth-promoters and other pharmaceutical preparations that are routinely administered to intensively reared livestock. Don't use salting or pickling as a way of disguising or prolonging the life of meat that is past its best.

Salt is the essential preservative in this curing process. It works by osmosis, drawing liquid out of the tissues of the meat. At the same time salt passes through the semi-permeable cell walls into the meat and this two-way traffic continues until the concentration of the pickling brine and the cell fluids is the same. The combination of salt in the tissues and the lack of moisture inhibits the growth of micro-organisms that would cause the meat to spoil and decay.

Salt also provides its own flavour, and for dry-salting and brining you should use good-quality rock salt or sea salt. Avoid common table salt, which is dull and normally includes anti-caking agents such as sodium hexacyanoferrate II to give it free-running qualities. These chemicals also slow down the rate at which the salt (sodium chloride) penetrates the tissues of meat.

Saltpetre, sodium nitrate and sal prunella (all different forms of nitrate) have been used in meat curing for more than a century and were doubtless present in the process before that, since sodium nitrate is a naturally occurring impurity of rock salt. Nitrates have two functions: they give the meat a rosy pink colour (without it the flesh looks murky grey-brown after curing) and they are broken down by bacteria in the meat to form nitrites, which are recognised as a way of preventing the growth of *Clostridium botulinum* – the organism that causes botulism poisoning. There is much debate about the safety of nitrites and possible links with stomach cancer (due to the formation of nitrosamines in the gut). As yet the links have not been positively proven on humans, but home-curers should be aware of the problem.

I have included small quantities of saltpetre in the following recipes. However, if you are making modest batches of salted or pickled meat and consuming the results within a few days, you can dispense with this ingredient if you wish.

White or brown sugar can be added to some curing mixtures. It provides flavour, counteracts any hardening of the flesh caused by the salt and also gives the meat some colour. Various herbs and spices can also be added to the salt or brine mixture as flavourings – and it's worth experimenting with different types.

2 Equipment

You will need a few special pieces of equipment for pickling meat in brine, but nothing too expensive or elaborate. A large stoneware crock is the basic item – although a white plastic bucket or dustbin will serve just as well. Other items include a pair of stainless-steel or plastic tongs for turning the meat while it is in the brine; a wooden spoon or stick kept clean and used only for stirring the brine; and a piece of wood that will fit inside the crock or bucket to keep the meat below the surface. Everything else you need – weighing scales and so on – is a standard kitchen item.

All that equipment must be thoroughly scrubbed and washed in boiling water, to which some washing soda has been added, before and after pickling.

3 Dry-salting

The normal ingredients for dry-salting meat are salt, saltpetre, herbs, spices and sometimes sugar, depending on the recipe. Once all the equipment has been thoroughly cleaned and the meat prepared for curing, you need to grind the dry ingredients with a pestle and mortar so that you have a fine mixture that can be rubbed into the meat with ease.

During salting you will need to check that the curing mixture is in contact with every part of the meat. Rub the joint every day with the sticky brine that forms and turn regularly. Throughout the process keep the whole mixture covered and stored in a cool airy place at a temperature of not more than 40°F (5°C).

When the meat is ready, remove from the brine, wipe off any excess liquid and spices and prepare for cooking.

4   Pickling in brine

Like dry-salting, pickling in brine normally requires salt, saltpetre, herbs, spices and sometimes sugar, depending on the recipe. Once all the equipment has been cleaned, dissolve the salt, saltpetre (and sugar, if using) in the required amount of water in a large pan and bring to the boil. Skim off any scum that rises to the surface. Add spices, herbs or other flavourings, simmer for a further 5 minutes, then remove from the heat and allow the brine to cool.

Strain the cooled brine into your crock or bucket, put in the meat and lay on top the piece of wood previously washed in boiling water. Cover and store in a cool place with an even temperature of not more than 40°F (5°C) for the required amount of time. The actual brining time varies from recipe to recipe and from meat to meat; it also depends as much on the thickness of the joint as on its weight. Stir the brine with a wooden spoon from time to time, and turn the meat using a pair of tongs. Once the meat is cured, take it out and leave it to drain before cooking.

If you are pickling meat for more than 4 days, the brine may become weaker – and less effective – as salt is absorbed. So it is a good idea to add some extra salt – say, 4 oz (100 g) – to counteract this.

Don't panic if some mould appears on the surface of the brine. Skim it off, remove the meat straight away and wash it well before cooking. Throw away the brine and clean all your equipment thoroughly before embarking on another pickling session. However, if you notice that the brine has become thick and viscous or the meat has turned slimy and has a strong, suspicious smell, it must be thrown away. Don't risk cooking or eating it.

It is possible to maintain a pickling brine for several months, but for small-scale curing it is better – and probably safer – to begin from scratch each time. Don't put different kinds of meat into the brine together as it will become contaminated and flavours will get confused.

5   Preparing to cook pickled meat

Before pickled meat is cooked it may need to be soaked in cold water to remove excess salt. This will depend on the length of time that the meat has been cured, and also on your own palate. Put the meat into a bowl of cold water and leave for about 15 minutes. Taste the water: if it is very salty, throw it away and soak the meat again in fresh water. A joint of 2–3 lb (1–1.5 kg) will need only 30 minutes' extra soaking, while a large leg or other joint may require more than 12 hours' soaking before it is ready for cooking.

The following recipes explain how to cure and then cook various meats. After the meat has been cooked, it should be wrapped in foil and stored in a cool place. Most types will keep for around 7 days.

SPICED BEEF

One of the great Victorian Christmas dishes, and a speciality that deserves to be revived with gusto. It makes the perfect centrepiece for a seasonal cold supper, especially if served with an ambitious selection of fruity pickles and relishes.

This recipe appeared in *The Perfect Pickle Book* (BBC Books, 1988), but spiced beef is such a seminal larder food that it deserves a place here as well.

Serves 10

6 lb (2.75 kg) joint silverside or topside of beef	1 oz (25 g) juniper berries
	1 oz (25 g) whole allspice
3 oz (75 g) light brown sugar	4 oz (100 g) sea salt
1 oz (25 g) black peppercorns	¼ oz (10 g) saltpetre

Trim the meat and tie into a neat round. Rub it all over with sugar, put into a large pot, cover with a lid and leave in a cool place for 2 days. Turn the meat occasionally and rub with the sticky liquor.

Crush the peppercorns, juniper berries and allspice with a pestle and mortar and mix with the salt and saltpetre. Rub this mixture well into the meat and leave in the pot for a further 9 days. During this time you must tend the beef every day, turning it and rubbing the pickle into the flesh.

When the pickling is complete, remove the beef from the pot and rub off any excess spices adhering to the surface. Do not rinse it. Wrap the meat in aluminium foil and put into a large lidded ovenproof dish. Add about 10 fl oz (300 ml) water, cover the top with a double layer of foil and fit on the lid tightly.

Pre-heat the oven to gas mark 1, 275°F (140°C). Bake the meat slowly, allowing 45 minutes per lb (450 g). When the meat is cooked, remove the dish from the oven and set aside until quite cold: this will take several hours. Unwrap the meat, drain off any excess liquor and put on to a board. Cover with a piece of foil, place a heavy weight on top and leave in a cool place for 24 hours. Carve into thin slices and serve with appropriate accompaniments. The beef should keep well for up to 7 days if wrapped in foil and stored in a cool place.

SALT MUTTON/LAMB

Very fat mutton may be salted to great advantage and may be kept for a long while. Not the shoulders and legs, but the back of the sheep. I have never made a flitch of 'sheep-bacon', but I will; for there is nothing like having a 'store' of meat in the house. The running to the butcher's daily is a ridiculous thing. The very idea of being 'fed', of a family being 'fed', has something in it perfectly tormenting. One half of the time of a mistress of the house, the affairs of which are carried on in this way, is taken up in talking about what is to be got for dinner, and in negotiations with the butcher. . . . To suffer a system of domestic economy which unnecessarily wastes an hour or two of the mistresses time in hunting for the provision of the repast is a shame indeed.

(From *Cottage Economy* by William Cobbett, 1824.)

Cobbett's idea of 'cottage economy' didn't imply frugality or austerity; it was simply 'the proper management of one's affairs'. Curing was essential to his notion of provisions and stores: it was the last link in a chain of self-sufficiency that stretched from the farmyard to the table.

These days mutton is scarce, but you can use a boned and rolled leg or shoulder of lamb instead. Choose fresh meat from a mature animal and follow the recipe given for Spiced Beef (page 37). Serve hot with caper sauce or, Welsh-style, with laverbread (cooked and prepared seaweed).

SALT DUCK

Almost every corner of Britain once had its own method of salting ducks, but this classic speciality is now confined to a few parts of Wales, where it is still very popular. Salt duck is normally cooked and eaten hot with onion sauce or a purée of onions enriched with butter. It also makes a splendid cold meal: Elizabeth David recommends serving slices of the meat with cubes of honeydew melon seasoned with lemon juice.

Always use a fresh duck for this dish, never a frozen one.

Serves 4 as a main course

1 large duck   4 oz (100 g) sea salt

Clean the duck well and remove the giblets. Rub it inside and out with sea salt and put into a deep dish. Cover and leave in a cool larder for 2–3 days. Rub the duck from time to time with the concentrated brine that forms during the curing process.

Once the duck is sufficiently salted, it is ready for cooking. Pre-heat the oven to gas mark 2, 300°F (150°C). Wash any excess salt off the bird and place it in a deep casserole dish that will easily contain it. Cover with water and put the dish into a large baking tin, which is about one third full of water. Cook in the oven for about 2 hours. Carve and serve.

PICKLED PORK

Pickling (or 'sousing') pork is a centuries-old tradition, dating back to the time when pigs were vital as a source of food in country households. The brine barrel was an essential part of every good larder and it was used for everything from belly and shoulder cuts to trotters and tails.

Pork was often left in the pickle (or 'sousing drink') right through the winter months to preserve it. These days, of course, we don't need to take such extreme measures, and pickled pork is a mild delicacy produced for its special flavour more than its keeping qualities. Any cut of pork can be used for pickling, and it is one of the simplest methods of preserving meat – provided that you follow the basic guidelines on pages 34–37.

Belly pork

Belly is the most versatile cut of all. Choose a slab about 2–3 lb (1–1.5 kg) to begin with. Select a piece with a good showing of fat – which holds most of the flavour after pickling – and don't bother to cut off the rind.

The traditional way of eating pickled pork is to simmer it slowly in spicy stock (allow about 20 minutes per pound). Serve with a purée of broad beans or split peas; it also goes well with a pile of haricot beans and steamed cabbage.

3 lb (1.5 kg) belly pork
12 oz (350 g) sea salt
1 oz (25 g) saltpetre
4 pints (2.25 litres) water
1 teaspoon (1 × 5 ml spoon)
   juniper berries

1 teaspoon (1 × 5 ml spoon)
   black peppercorns
1 teaspoon (1 × 5 ml spoon)
   whole allspice
4 oz (100 g) soft brown sugar
   (optional)

Wash and clean all your pickling equipment thoroughly, then make up the brine as described on page 36. A small amount of brown sugar gives the meat an extra flavour, adds colour and also counteracts any hardening caused by the salt in the brine.

When the brine is cool, put in the meat and, to keep it submerged, place on top a piece of wood which you have washed well in boiling water. Stir the brine occasionally with a wooden spoon and turn the meat using tongs rather than by delving your hands into the brine. Leave for 3 days. Then remove the meat with tongs and leave it to drain. It is now ready for cooking.

Hand of pork

This corresponds to the fore-knuckle and fore-hock of bacon. Get the butcher to bone and roll a joint weighing about 5 lb (2.25 kg). Pickle in brine for 5–6 days in the usual way (see page 36). A joint like this is ideal for slow-baking in the oven. Cook at gas mark 3, 325°F (160°C), allowing 30 minutes per pound (450 g). It is equally good eaten hot or cold.

Leg of pork

A whole leg of pork can be put into brine for 12 hours to season it before roasting.

Alternatively you can bone and roll the meat and pickle it for about 10 days, depending on its thickness and weight. Then it can be used to produce what the French call *jambon blanc* or *jambon de Paris*. Tie the pickled leg in a cloth, simmer in a pan of water with carrots, onions and herbs, allowing 30 minutes per pound (450 g). Allow it to cool, then press it as described for Spiced Beef (page 37) and eat cold.

Trotters

Pigs' trotters are cheap and are greatly improved by being lightly pickled. Hind trotters have the most meat on them, but all are suitable for curing. Wash and scrub them, scraping off any hairs, then put into brine for 24–48 hours before cooking. They will need about 2 hours' slow simmering.

In Ireland, pickled trotters (known as 'crubeens') are eaten in pubs on Saturday night with soda bread and pints of heavy stout. Boiled pigs' trotters are versatile: they can add flavour, body and richness to stocks, stews and casseroles; they can be served hot with mashed potatoes and onion sauce; they can be split when cold and the pieces put into a salad with chopped tongue, hard-boiled eggs, parsley and a garlicky vinaigrette; the morsels of gelatinous meat can also be dipped in egg and breadcrumbs and deep-fried.

Ears and tails

The ears and tail of the pig are often wasted or consigned to sausages and brawns, but a good butcher should be able to let you have some cheaply. They need to be scalded, thoroughly cleaned and singed to remove any dirt or hairs before being put into brine for 24–48 hours.

Ears can be cooked like trotters, simmered for 1–1½ hours (see above), then flattened out under a weight, dipped in egg and breadcrumbs and fried. They go well with a soup or purée of red lentils or split peas. Pickled tails should be simmered very gently for at least 2 hours or until the meat falls from the chain of tiny bones.

BATH CHAPS

Chaps, the cheek pieces of the pig, became well known as a delicacy in Bath during the eighteenth century. Bath chaps were originally produced from long-jawed Gloucester Old Spot pigs that fed on windfalls from the local apple orchards. Old Spots are making a comeback, thanks to the efforts of the Rare Breeds Survival Trust and a few enterprising West Country farmers.

Bath chaps are cooked and eaten cold with pickles, strong English mustard and potatoes, or they can be served hot accompanied by pease pudding and parsley sauce.

Serves 4

2 chaps
4 oz (100 g) sea salt

4 pints (2.25 litres) pickling brine
  (see page 36)

To serve hot:

10 fl oz (300 ml) unsalted meat
  or vegetable stock
10 fl oz (300 ml) dry cider
8 oz (225 g) selection of root
  vegetables, chopped
bunch of herbs

To serve cold:

toasted breadcrumbs

Get the butcher to prepare and trim the chaps for you. Wash and clean them well, rub all over with sea salt, put into a shallow stainless-steel dish and leave in a cool place for 24 hours.

Make up a pickling brine as described on page 36. Wipe the excess salt from the chaps, then put them into the pickle. Cover with a piece of wood, which you have washed in boiling water, so that they are submerged and leave for 2–3 days depending on the size of the chaps. Turn from time to time.

Remove from the brine and leave to drain. Then simmer for about 2 hours in a mixture of 50/50 unsalted stock and dry cider with root vegetables and herbs. Before serving, discard any tiny bones.

If you want to eat the chaps cold, they should be skinned, pressed under a weight for a couple of hours, then rolled in toasted breadcrumbs and carved into slices. The cooked chaps should be eaten within 3 days.

PICKLED BEEF

'It is tough, hard, heavy, and ill of nourishment, requiring rather the stomach of another Hercules than of any ordinary common ploughman.' That is how Thomas Muffett described 'salt beef' in 1655. In those days the meat was either 'powdered' (dry-salted) or pickled in brine. In either case it was an essential provision for farm workers and sailors on long sea voyages.

Thankfully today's salt beef is more attractive. It may not be refined, but it has a special delicate flavour because of the mild pickling in brine. First choose your meat: both silverside and brisket are excellent for pickling. Silverside is a quite expensive lean cut that is ideal for baking and eating cold, cut into large thin slices. Brisket is cheaper, layered with fat (which adds flavour and stops the meat from becoming too dry when it is cooked), and it is best boiled and eaten hot. Pickled brisket is the starting point for that classic London dish, boiled beef and carrots.

Serves 10

5 lb (2.25 kg) joint silverside or brisket of beef	2 sprigs thyme
12 oz (350 g) sea salt	1 teaspoon (1 × 5 ml spoon) black peppercorns
1 oz (25 g) saltpetre	1 teaspoon (1 × 5 ml spoon) cloves
4 pints (2.25 litres) water	
1 bay leaf	

Tie the meat into a firm round shape so that it will carve easily. Make up a brine as described on page 36 and add the herbs and spices. Pickle the beef for about 7 days; larger joints will need 2–3 days longer. Keep the meat submerged with a piece of wood which you have washed in boiling water and turn from time to time. Remove from the brine, allow to drain and cook in any way you wish. (If the beef is too salty for your taste, it can be soaked for a few hours before cooking – see page 36.)

Once the meat is cooked it can be eaten hot, or pressed and eaten cold – in which case it should be used within 5 days.

PICKLED OX TONGUE

In the days when autumn slaughtering was part of rural economy, the Martinmas ox provided both fresh and cured meat. One of the essentials was the tongue, which was normally pickled in brine. Large 'neats' tongues', as they were called, were put in the brine barrel for up to 3 weeks, but these days ox tongues are smaller and the curing is much milder.

Pickled tongues are common in butchers' shops – especially at Christmas time – but it is very simple to make your own at home. Once the tongue has been cured and cooked, it can be served hot in thick slices with a fruity sauce made from currants or Morello cherries, or pressed and eaten cold with salad, pickles and mustard.

Serves 10

1 × 5–6 lb (2.25–2.75 kg) fresh ox tongue
12 oz (350 g) sea salt
1 oz (25 g) saltpetre
1 teaspoon (1 × 5 ml spoon) black peppercorns
1 teaspoon (1 × 5 ml spoon) whole allspice
2 bay leaves
4 pints (2.25 litres) water

To serve hot:

2 onions stuck with a few cloves
a few carrots, chopped
1 bunch mixed fresh herbs

Soak the tongue for a few hours in a bowl of cold water to remove any excess blood. Take it out, let it drain, then prick the skin all over with a clean needle.

Prepare the brine as described on page 36. Put in the tongue and leave for about 5 days. (Smaller tongues will need less time in the brine.) Remove from the brine, wash in clean water and allow to drain. If you wish to cook the tongue, it will need to be soaked in cold water for up to 12 hours beforehand to remove excess salt, then drained.

To cook, put the drained tongue into a large saucepan, cover with water and bring to the boil. Remove any scum that forms, then reduce the heat to a simmer. Add the whole onions stuck with cloves, the chopped carrots and the herbs. Cover the pan and cook very slowly for 3–4 hours depending on the size of the tongue.

When it is fully cooked, lift out the tongue and leave it to cool. Trim off any excess fat, gristle or tiny bones at the throat end, then slit the underside lengthways and carefully strip off the skin. If you want to eat the tongue hot, slice it thickly and serve.

If you want to eat the tongue cold, you will need to press it. A cake tin with a removable base is very handy for this. Curl the skinned tongue into the tin, cover with a piece of aluminium foil and a plate or board that will just fit inside the tin. Weight it down and leave in a cool place for 24 hours. When the tongue is thoroughly pressed, turn it out and it is ready to serve. A pickled tongue should keep well in a cool place for 7–10 days.

CHAPTER FOUR

SAUSAGES

According to the *Concise Oxford English Dictionary* a sausage is 'pork or other meat, minced, seasoned and stuffed into long cylindrical cases prepared from entrails and divided when full into lengths of a few inches by twisting or tying'. No doubt this curious idea was devised by our Neolithic ancestors who wanted some way of preserving meat from the animals they hunted. Their solution was to chop up the flesh, flavour it with herbs and berries from the surrounding countryside, then stuff the whole lot into the cleaned intestines of the animals. A convenient package like this could be hung over an open fire to cure and the meat then didn't go bad.

Most ancient civilisations developed their own variations on this theme, but the Romans paved the way for today's sausages; their word *salsicium* (meaning something salted) suggests that most of their products were made with salted and pickled meat, but they also made fresh and smoked sausages and blood puddings, all heavily flavoured with herbs and spices. Once in Britain, the Romans continued to produce sausages – in fact some archaeologists think that there was a fully fledged sausage factory in Verulamium, the town now known as St Albans.

British sausages followed in due course. Various kinds of meat were used, but pork was the first choice. Pigs were the great all-purpose food animals of the Middle Ages, providing bacon, hams and other products: their blood went for black puddings, while scraps of flesh found their way into sausages whose skins were made from the animals' intestines. Before long there were also 'white' puddings (tinged yellow with saffron), sausages sweetened with currants and sugar, and others made from pigs' liver enriched with cream. By the seventeenth century sausages were being twisted into the now familiar links which were hung up 'in the corner of some chimney clean swept' to take on a mild smoky flavour, or kept in the larder until required for boiling, grilling or stewing.

During the eighteenth and nineteenth centuries, sausage stalls were a common sight on fairgrounds – like today's hot-dog and burger stands – and well-organised sausage parlours dispensed their home-produced wares in London. But in the second half of the nineteenth century, as the Industrial Revolution gained momentum and transport improved, sausages went into mass-production. Newspapers and advertising helped spread the word, and factories began to churn out 'bangers' by the ton, often despatching them to towns and cities hundreds of miles away.

That legacy is still with us in Britain, and it is little wonder that our sausages have been abused and criticised over the years. Today's laws require pork sausages to contain a minimum of 65 per cent 'meat' (the figure is 50 per cent for beef), but only half of this has to be conventional 'lean' meat; the rest can be fat or any bit of the animal that could be construed as 'meat' – gizzards, head meat, stomach, testicles, udder and worse. There are also no legal controls on 'mechanically recovered meat' (MRM) – obtained by pulping or scraping off any bits of meat attached to bone – and this may find its way into commercially produced sausages.

That is not all, however. Factory sausages can contain as much as 20 per cent cereal or rusk as a binder, to stop the meat in the sausage from falling apart. Then there are the additives: colourings to make the sausages look meaty and 'appetising', preservatives to stop them going bad and allow them to be conveniently distributed and stored in bulk over long periods, monosodium glutamate or other 'flavour enhancers' to mask blandness, and polyphosphates to enable the meat to hold plenty of water. Commercial sausage-makers are trying to improve their act and are appearing to respond to consumer pressure. But even if they decide to remove, say, preservatives from their products, the results are still far from wholesome. British sausage-makers should follow the example of countries such as France and Germany, where it is illegal to include anything but prime lean meat and fat, and both cereals and additives are outlawed.

Given this state of affairs, making your own sausages is more than just an eccentric pastime. The impetus to do it yourself goes hand in hand with quality: you have control over the ingredients and the process from start to finish. You don't need to imitate factory methods, which means that you can use good-quality meat with just enough fat to make the sausages moist; in most cases you can dispense with cereal binder and breadcrumbs altogether. Fresh herbs and seasonings are in, artificial additives are out.

GUIDELINES FOR MAKING SAUSAGES

1 Hygiene

Handling quantities of raw meat, particularly pork, together with chopping, mincing and mixing all the other ingredients, means that there is always the risk of contamination unless you are careful. So follow the basic rules of kitchen hygiene. Keep your hands clean and well washed after each stage in the process; make sure that all your kitchen equipment is thoroughly scrubbed in boiling water before you start and again when you finish sausage-making.

2 Equipment

The essential piece of equipment for sausage-making is a filler attachment, which can be fitted to an electric mixer, mincing machine or food processor. Sausage skins *can* be filled by hand using a funnel, but this is frustrating and hopelessly messy. You can also purchase domestic-sized sausage-making machines from some good catering and kitchen equipment shops. Or write direct to: Catermasters Ltd, West Street, Dunster, Somerset TA24 6SN.

3 Chopping and mincing

Whether you chop or mince the meat (or both) depends on the kind of sausage or sausagemeat you are making. If you want a really coarse texture, chopping is the answer. Use an old-style square-bladed English chopper, a crescent-shaped French *hachoir* or a heavy sharp knife. Any of these will do the job.

Mincing can be done with an old-fashioned hand mincer which has different-sized holes in its metal plates. For most susages with a fine texture this is the best – though not the quickest – method. If you want speed, use an electric mixer or food processor with variable settings so that you can control the process. Mincing does have one disadvantage: it tends to squeeze juices out of the meat.

4 The filling

Sausage fillings are normally a mixture of meat, poultry or game (very occasionally fish) with added flavourings and seasonings.

There is one golden rule: the better the meat, the better the sausage. Of course, you don't need to fill sausages with the very best pork tenderloin, but you should avoid rough scraps, trimmings, lumps of gristle and so on. Sausages can be made from virtually any kind of meat – from pork, beef and lamb to turkey and venison; it can be fresh, salted, pickled or smoked and you can blend together all manner of different combinations. If possible, use meat from animals that have been naturally reared without growth promoters or other drugs. The flavour of pork from a mature, free-range pig or of well-hung, organically produced beef is incomparable.

All sausages need some fat to keep them moist. Hard back fat from the pig or fat from unsmoked streaky bacon are the most common. The proportion of lean to fat depends on the type of sausage and the recipe.

British manufacturers continue to use cereals and binders in their mass-produced sausages to bulk out the mixture and to stop it from crumbling and falling apart. But remember that if the meat is really fresh it will bind together naturally; the staler it is, the less it will absorb water and the less it will bind – which is another reason for using good meat. If you are making sausages on a small scale, you can add a little beaten egg or breadcrumbs, although this isn't really essential.

All kinds of herbs are used in sausages, from sage to basil. Use fresh herbs if possible, otherwise substitute dried, remembering that 1 teaspoon (5 ml) dried herbs is equivalent to approximately 3 teaspoons (15 ml) fresh. Spices should be freshly ground if possible, as they have the best flavour. Black – and sometimes white – pepper are essential, but many other spices, from coriander to paprika, appear in different recipes. Variety, spice and experiment are the name of the game. Use sea or rock salt as a seasoning rather than table salt, which has a poor flavour and usually contains additives to make it 'free-running'.

To check that your sausage filling is seasoned correctly, fry a small ball of the mixture until it is cooked through and taste it; you can then adjust the seasoning as necessary.

5   The skin

Almost all sausages come in a skin – or casing – which can be natural or man-made. Natural skins are by far the best and give the best results. They are the intestines of sheep, pigs and cattle, which are cleaned, purified and salted using an elaborate technical process. Preference for natural skins isn't simply a matter of sentimentality: natural skins actually work better than artificial ones. They are stronger, easier to digest and contribute to the flavour of the sausage; they cook better and have less tendency to burst, and they are permeable. They also allow the sausages to be linked together without folds or bits of unfilled skin at the end.

Man-made (collagen) casings are produced by chemically reprocessing the inner fatty membrane of cattle hides. Sausage manufacturers like them because they have a constant diameter and thickness. Commercial sausages with man-made skins tend to be straight and even; natural skins produce a sausage that is gently curved in shape.

Man-made skins are supplied in batches too large for most households and they are generally inferior. Find a supplier of natural skins (see below), and decide what size skin you need. For most domestic purposes, sheeps' or pigs' intestines are suitable; others, such as those from cows, are too large and unwieldy for use at home. As a rough guide, 1 lb (450 g) sausages will require about 3 ft (90 cm) of skins. Natural skins are normally processed and salted, so before use they need to be soaked in a bowl of water for 30 minutes to soften them. Prior to soaking it is a good idea to fit the end of the skin over the tap and run cold water through it to check if there are any holes or splits, which might ruin your sausages.

Skins can be obtained direct from Gysin & Hanson Ltd, 96 Trundleys Road, London SE8 5JG (they supply a domestic pack with skins, herbs, recipes and instructions); and from Smallholding Supplies, Pikes Farmhouse, East Pennard, Shepton Mallet, Somerset BA4 6RR (their free catalogue also lists other accessories for the kitchen and larder).

Alternatively, take the easy way out. If you have a friendly local butcher, you may be able to buy a small batch of skins from him. He may also be willing to fill the skins with your own sausage mixture for a small charge, using his own machine.

6   The basic filling method

(a) Soak the natural skins in a bowl of water for 30 minutes. Drain and pat dry with a clean cloth.

(b) Prepare the sausagemeat mixture following the recipe of your choice. Chop or mince the meat to the required consistency and texture. At this stage it is a good idea to fry a little of the mixture and taste it to test the seasoning and flavour. You can then adjust this if necessary.

(c) Set up your sausage-making machine according to the instructions, or fit the filler attachment to your mixer.

(d) Tie a knot in one end of the skin. Open up the other end and slide most of it on to the nozzle; if it has been well soaked, it should slide on quite easily. Leave the other end 1–2 inches (2.5–5 cm) from the nozzle, ready for the first meat to arrive.

(e) Start the machine and control the filling and flow with your hands. (A second pair of hands is a help when guiding the filled sausage on to a tray or dish.) Go slowly at first and adjust the speed if necessary. Remember that by controlling how fast the casing comes off the nozzle you can vary the thickness of the sausage. Don't overfill the skins or they will burst when cooked. Squeeze out any air as you proceed.

(f) Once the sausage skin is filled, remove it from the nozzle and tie a knot in the other end. Then you can leave it in one continuous length or twist it into 'links' as required. Pinch and twist the sausage at about 4 inch (10 cm) intervals: this will give you six to eight sausages to the lb (450 g), depending on the thickness of the filling.

Put the sausages on to a plate or hang them up in a cool larder overnight for the flavours to mature and develop.

7   Storing

If you are keeping your sausages in a cool larder, they need to be eaten within 2–3 days, depending on the recipe. Transfer them to a fridge if you need to keep them any longer, but remember that they will not keep as long as commercially produced sausages because they contain no preservatives.

Sausages can be frozen in batches for 1–2 months, but make sure that they are properly thawed before you use them.

Cooked sausages can also be preserved in fat, like French *confits*. In *Charcuterie and French Pork Cookery* (Penguin, 1970) Jane Grigson suggests that sausages are gently sautéed in lard until golden-brown, then packed in sterilised stoneware pots or large bottling jars. They are covered with melted lard to a depth of at least ½ inch (1 cm) above the highest sausage. When the lard has solidified, it can be covered with aluminium foil and the whole lot will keep perfectly well in a cool place for several weeks. Although a few sausages can be used and the jar re-sealed, it is much safer to use a whole batch once it has been opened.

OXFORD SAUSAGE

If you want to know what the sausages of the past tasted like, here's a fascinating recipe from Hannah Glasse's *The Art of Cookery Made Plain and Easy* (1796 edition). You can follow it to the letter if you want an authentic result, or adapt it to suit your taste: the quantities of beef suet and 'grated bread', in particular, might seem excessive nowadays.

This is a sausage without a skin, and the meat mixture was meant to be preserved: the directions to 'put close down in a pan' refer to potting and storing the mixture until needed.

Take a pound of lean veal [450 g] of lean veal, a pound [450 g] of young pork, fat and lean, free from skin and gristle, a pound [450 g] of beef suet, chopped all fine together; put in half a pound [225 g] of grated bread, half a peel of a lemon shred fine, a nutmeg grated, six sage leaves washed and chopped very fine, a teaspoonful [1 × 5 ml spoon] of pepper and two [2 × 5 ml spoons] of salt, some thyme, savory, and marjoram shred fine; mix it all well together and put it close down in a pan: when you use it, roll it out the size of a common sausage and fry them in a butter of a fine brown, or broil them over a clear fire, and send them to the table as hot as possible.

PORK SAUSAGE

An all-purpose recipe for a genuine British sausage with plenty of lean meat. You can vary the herbs as you please. This is the sausage for 'bangers and mash', served with strong English mustard, fried onions and gravy.

Makes 2½ lb (1.25 kg)

2 lb (1 kg) lean pork
8 oz (225 g) belly pork
2 teaspoons (2 × 5 ml spoons)
  chopped fresh sage

2 teaspoons (2 × 5 ml spoons)
  chopped fresh thyme
sea salt and freshly ground black
  pepper to taste

Trim the meat, discarding any bits of gristle, bone and rind. Chop into pieces, then put through a mincer. Mix the minced pork with the freshly chopped herbs. Season cautiously with salt and generously with freshly ground black pepper. Check the seasoning (see page 49) and adjust as necessary.

Fill into skins and divide into links in the usual way. Leave overnight in a cool place to allow the flavour to develop. Use within 2 days.

PORK, APPLE AND SAGE SAUSAGE

The Roebuck in Brimfield is a four-square black-and-white-painted hostelry on the border of Hereford and Worcester and Shropshire. Carole and John Evans run it as the local village pub with an inventive modern restaurant attached. Carole is renowned for her pickles and chutneys, but that is just the beginning. She now produces a whole range of larder foods, including her own mustards and sausages.

This is Carole's classic breakfast sausage. She suggests that the apple can be replaced with 4 oz (100 g) fine breadcrumbs if you want something that is not quite so rich and meaty to start the day.

Makes about 3 lb (1.5 kg)

2 lb (1 kg) lean shoulder pork
1 lb (450 g) hard back fat (pork)
1 large cooking apple, peeled, finely chopped and cored

1 tablespoon (1 × 15 ml spoon) finely chopped fresh sage
sea salt to taste

For the mixed spices:

2 oz (50 g) ground white pepper
½ oz (15 g) ground ginger
½ oz (15 g) ground nutmeg or cinnamon

1 teaspoon (1 × 5 ml spoon) ground cloves

Trim the meat, discarding any bone, rind or gristle. Chop into pieces and mince coarsely. Add the apple and sage, plus 2 teaspoons (2 × 5 ml spoons) of the mixed spices and some salt. Check the seasoning (see page 49) and adjust as necessary.

Fill the mixture into skins and divide into links in the usual way. Leave in a cool place to allow the flavour to mature and use within 2 days.

PORK SAUSAGE WITH PISTACHIO NUTS

A pork sausage with a difference. The pistachio nuts provide colour and give the sausages an unusual texture.

Makes about 2½ lb (1.25 kg)

2 lb (1 kg) lean pork
8 oz (225 g) belly pork
2 cloves garlic, crushed

4 oz (100 g) pistachio nuts,
    shelled
sea salt and freshly ground black
    pepper to taste

Trim the meat, discarding any bits of rind, gristle or bone. Chop into pieces, then mince well. Mix the minced meat with the garlic.

Soak the pistachio nuts in boiling water for 15 minutes, then drain well and rub off the skins – they should come away easily. Grind the nuts or chop into tiny pieces and add to the meat. Season with sea salt and black pepper to taste (see page 49 for how to check the seasoning).

Fill into skins and divide into links in the usual way. Leave overnight in a cool place to allow the flavour to develop and use within 2 days.

CUMBERLAND SAUSAGE

The great feature of a genuine Cumberland sausage is its length. It is not divided up into links and you buy it by the inch, not by the pound. The real thing still appears in some butchers' shops in the Lake District, meticulously coiled like thick rope or draped from hooks in huge loops. Commercial manufacturers have taken up the name, but most of their products are pale imitations, sold eight to the pound. Cumberland sausage should be coarse and meaty, without being dry; it should also be strongly spiced with black pepper, although most versions do not include herbs.

This is a solid sausage, so fry it slowly, then crisp up the skin at the last moment. Serve with red cabbage, fried apple rings or Yorkshire pudding.

Makes 3 lb (1.5 kg)

2½ lb (1.25 kg) lean pork
8 oz (225 g) belly pork
pinch of sea salt

1–2 teaspoons (1–2 × 5 ml
  spoons) freshly ground black
  pepper

Trim the meat, discarding any bits of gristle, bone or rind. Chop into pieces, then mince coarsely: the texture needs to be rough. Add a pinch of sea salt and freshly ground black pepper to suit your taste (see page 49 for how to check the seasoning).

Fill the sausage mixture into skins in the normal way, but do not divide up into links. Coil the mixture on to a plate and store overnight in a cool place to allow the flavour to develop. Use within 2 days.

BEEF AND TOMATO SAUSAGE

Tomato sausages are well known in the Midlands and North of England, but are usually made from pork. This recipe is a good way of brightening up the otherwise rather dull beef sausage and it makes use of cheaper cuts of beef such as skirt.

Makes 3 lb (1.5 kg)

2 lb (1 kg) beef skirt
1 lb (450 g) belly pork
1 tablespoon (1 × 15 ml spoon)
  tomato purée

2 teaspoons (2 × 5 ml spoons)
  chopped fresh basil
sea salt and freshly ground black
  pepper to taste

Trim the meat, discarding any gristle, sinew, bone and rind. Chop into pieces, then mince well. Mix in a bowl with the tomato purée and basil. Season lightly with sea salt and strongly with black pepper. Check the seasoning (see page 49) and adjust as necessary.

Fill into skins and divide into links in the usual way. Store overnight in a cool place to let the flavour mature. Use within 3 days.

LAMB AND MINT SAUSAGE

Roast lamb with mint sauce is a famous pairing, and the same combination also works well in a sausage. For the best results use fresh mint.

Makes 3 lb (1.5 kg)

2 lb (1 kg) neck or shoulder of lamb
8 oz (225 g) lean pork
8 oz (225 g) belly pork

2 teaspoons (2 × 5 ml spoons) chopped fresh mint
sea salt and freshly ground black pepper to taste

Trim the lamb and pork, discarding any bone, skin, gristle and rind. Chop into pieces and mince well. Add the mint and season with salt and pepper. Check the seasoning (see page 49) and adjust as necessary.

Fill into skins and divide into links in the usual way. Store in a cool place overnight to allow the flavour to mature and use within 2 days.

VENISON SAUSAGE

Another recipe from Carole Evans at the Roebuck, Brimfield. Use cheap cuts of venison if possible or a mixture of trimmings, depending on what the butcher can offer you. The venison needs to be marinated to tenderise it and improve its flavour.

Makes about 4½ lb (2 kg)

2 lb (1 kg) shoulder of venison
1 lb (450 g) venison rump trimmings
5 fl oz (150 ml) red wine
5 fl oz (150 ml) dark rum
1½ lb (750 g) hard back fat (pork)
2 cloves garlic
1 large Cox's apple, cored (but not peeled) and grated
2 teaspoons (2 × 5 ml spoons) juniper berries, crushed

1½ teaspoons (1½ × 5 ml spoons) ground ginger
1 teaspoon (1 × 5 ml spoon) ground mace
1 tablespoon (1 × 15 ml spoon) chopped fresh sage
1 tablespoon (1 × 15 ml spoon) chopped fresh parsley
sea salt and freshly ground black pepper to taste

Trim the meat, discarding any gristle or bone. Put into a non-metallic bowl and cover with the wine and rum. Leave to marinate in a cool place for 24 hours. Remove the meat from the marinade and mince coarsely. Remove any rind from the back fat and discard. Mince the fat and mix with the meat. Add the garlic, apple, spices and herbs and mix well. Season with salt and pepper to taste: check the seasoning (see page 49) and adjust as necessary.

Fill the sausage into skins and divide into links in the usual way. Store overnight in a cool place to let the flavour mature. Use within 4 days.

TOULOUSE SAUSAGE

The world is full of good sausages – hundreds, even thousands of different types, from scores of countries. British sausages can be excellent if properly made, the Germans claim they produce the best *wurst* of all, and both the Italians and French also have a prodigious range.

Toulouse sausages are well known in France and are widely available. They are big and hefty, made from lean and fat pork roughly chopped by hand and slightly sweetened with sugar. Some recipes include saltpetre, which gives the meat a characteristic pink colour, but this is not essential. Use Toulouse sausages in cassoulets and casseroles, or grill them and eat with hot potato salad.

Makes 2 lb (1 kg)

1½ lb (750 g) lean pork	2 teaspoons (2 × 5 ml spoons)
8 oz (225 g) hard back fat (pork)	white sugar
1 tablespoon (1 × 15 ml spoon)	freshly ground black pepper to
sea salt	taste

Trim the meat and discard any bone, gristle or rind. Chop coarsely with a knife or cleaver (do not mince). Put the meat in a bowl with the seasonings, mix well, cover and leave in a cool place overnight.

Next day mix again and check the seasoning (see page 49), adjusting as necessary, then fill into large skins in the usual way. Divide up into big links – so that each sausage weighs about 4 oz (100 g). Store overnight in a cool place so that the flavour has a chance to develop fully. Use within 2 days.

HAGGIS

Haggis is one of the curiosities of the sausage family. It's a large ball-shaped speciality whose skin is the belly (or paunch) of a sheep. The skin is stuffed with a mixture of oatmeal, suet, minced liver, heart and lights, all heavily seasoned.

There are plenty of good haggis-makers in Scotland if you don't wish to embark on the task of making your own. Try Macsween's of 13 Bruntsfield Place, Edinburgh EH10 4ES, and Ian Miller of Jamesfield Farm, Newburgh, Fife KY14 6EW (who makes his haggis from organically produced ingredients). Both can supply by mail order.

However, if you are intrigued, here is the classic method based on a recipe first described by one Mrs MacIver in Edinburgh in 1787. The traditional accompaniments to haggis have not changed over the years: creamed potatoes and mashed turnips ('tatties and neeps'), plus a few drams of good malt whisky.

Wash a sheep's belly, scrape and clean it thoroughly. Let it stand overnight in cold water. Clean the sheep's pluck [heart, lungs and liver], put in a pan of boiling water and boil for 2 hours with the windpipe hanging out so that any drips can run into a basin below. Leave in the liquid overnight.

Cut off the windpipe, chop up the heart, liver and lights (lungs) and mix with 4 oz (100 g) suet and 1 lb (450 g) chopped onions. Toast 8 oz (225 g) pinhead oatmeal, mix with the other ingredients and season well with herbs, salt and plenty of pepper. Add some water if the mixture is too dry. Pack into the sheep's bag so that it is just over half-full. Sew up and tie the end well. Place in boiling water and simmer for 3 hours, pricking the skin occasionally to prevent the haggis from bursting.

(Adapted from *Cookery and Pastry* by Susanna MacIver,
Edinburgh, 1787.)

CHAPTER FIVE

COOKED MEAT PRODUCTS

Dish it on a plate in a fair clean dish, then put a rosemary branch on the top being first dipped in the white of an egg well beaten to froth . . . or a sprig of rosemary gilt with gold; the brawn spotted also with gold and silver leaves, or let your sprig be of a straight sprig of yew tree, or a straight furze bush, and put about the brawn stuck round with bay leaves three ranks round, and spotted with red and yellow jelly about the dish sides, also the same jelly and some of the brawn leached [sliced], jagged or cut with tin moulds, and carved lemons, oranges and barberries, bay-leaves gilt, red beets, pickled barberries, pickled gooseberries, or pickled grapes.

(From *The Accomplished Cook* by Robert May, 1687 edition.)

Believe it or not, that was the way cooks presented brawn in the seventeenth century. From the Middle Ages onwards many such cooked meats were ceremonial foods, given elaborate treatment as festive centrepieces. Brawns and boars' heads were just the beginning. There were also fantastic galantines – whole birds or pieces of meat which were boned but left intact with the skin attached and filled with an extravagant mixture of minced meat, strips of tongue, truffles, eggs and so on, and then tied up, boiled, glazed and decorated. Add to this potted game and fish, pickled and pressed meats, and you get some idea of the lavish range and invention of these products.

Of course, there was another side to the picture. The farmhouse tradition was more modest, but just as enterprising. At the centre of it was the pig. Every bit of the animal was used in some way – there was bacon and ham, black puddings made from its blood and brawn from its head. Trotters, ears and tail would go into the pickling barrel, and some of the meat was eaten fresh, as was an assortment of offal and bits and pieces that were used for faggots and other useful larder provisions.

Cottage economy and household management based on the pig have disappeared, but the carnivorous tradition still lives on, especially in the North of England. You have only to visit market stalls in Derby or Bolton or Bradford to see the range of cooked meats that still survive. And remember – most of these products are home-made. The vast array on some stalls can be a bewildering sight: above your head are strings of black puddings; in front of you lie trays with huge lumps of cooked liver and ox heart, pressed meats in slices or moulds, jellied veal, faggots, brawn, tongue and brisket. Some stalls specialise in tripe, chitterlings and cow heel, and occasionally you will find elder – cooked and pressed cow's udder, pale fawn in colour with a ring of golden jelly around it.

Most stalls sell roughly the same range of meats, but no two will taste alike. Each one will have its own distinctive character. That's the beauty of home-made provisions. And, of course, there are no additives to be found in most of these foods. What a contrast to the factory-produced cooked meats sold in most delicatessens, with their preservatives, artificial colourings and polyphosphates!

GUIDELINES FOR PREPARING COOKED MEAT PRODUCTS

1 Always use good-quality meat. It doesn't need to be from prime cuts, but it shouldn't be scraps or rubbish either.

2 Cooking should be slow and long. Don't be tempted to rush this part of the process, otherwise the meat will be tough and stringy. For most items it should be very soft and tender, without being sloppy or flavourless.

3 Remember that cold foods generally have less flavour than hot, so use spices, herbs and seasonings generously. But be careful with salt – especially if some of the ingredients are already salted or pickled.

4   In most cases you should chop the meat into reasonable-sized pieces. Mincing – especially with brawns and similar dishes – produces bland, pasty results, totally unlike the real thing.

5   You can produce the jellied stock needed for some meat products with the help of gelatine, but better results and a finer flavour come from bones, cow heel or pigs' trotters. The more you reduce and concentrate the stock, the better it will set – but don't go too far otherwise the taste will be extremely salty. To get a good 'set' you need to leave the dish in a cool place for at least 24 hours. Don't be impatient.

6   If you are potting the meat into a dish or mould, it is a good idea to wet the inside first. This makes turning out easier.

7   Most of these items are not for long keeping. They should be eaten within 2–3 days from the larder, but will keep a little longer if stored in the refrigerator. Dishes that include pickled or cured meat will keep for up to 7 days.

Note: Other cooked meats, such as Spiced Beef and Bath Chaps, are covered in Chapter Three.

BRAWN

The word 'brawn' in Middle English ('brawne' or 'braune') simply meant meat or fleshy muscle. The starting material was usually a pig's head, although other parts of this highly prized animal were also included. In the Middle Ages, brawn rose to fame and was the favoured centrepiece for festive occasions, heavily glazed, gilded and decorated with all manner of herbs and fruit. But its glory didn't last, and by the nineteenth century it was beginning to get a reputation as a cheap food, made from any bits and pieces that were available. This is a great pity, for good brawn is handsome, especially when served with mustard or Oxford Brawn Sauce (see page 120) and garnished with pickled eggs and pickled walnuts.

Robust regional variations have sprung up over the years: sheep's head, cow heel and even rabbit are turned into brawns – especially in north-east England and Scotland. Incidentally, brawn is sometimes called 'head cheese' – a reference to the fact that the meat was often put under a cheese press to set and solidify.

Makes about 2 lb (1 kg)

½ pig's head
1 salted pork hock
2 pig's trotters
2 bay leaves
1 sprig each parsley, thyme and
   sage

2 teaspoons (2 × 5 ml spoons)
   black peppercorns
1 teaspoon (1 × 5 ml spoon)
   cloves

Get the butcher to split and prepare the pig's head for you. Wash it well, together with the hock and trotters, then soak overnight in a bowl of cold water. Drain off the liquid and put the meat into a very large saucepan with all the other ingredients and cover with cold water. Bring to the boil, cover the pan and simmer for about 4 hours until the meat falls from the bone.

Lift out the head, hock and trotters. Remove any bones, skin and gristle (save them for the stock) and chop the flesh into small, neat pieces. Skin and slice the tongue to give variation in colour and texture. Pack the meat into a dish or mould, leaving enough space at the top for the concentrated stock.

Put the bones and trimmings back into the cooking liquid in the pan, bring to the boil again and simmer for 30 minutes. Strain the stock and spoon a little of it over the meat to form a glistening layer on top. Leave to cool, then press under a weighted board for 24 hours. Store in a cool place and eat within 3 days.

FAGGOTS (1)

There's some debate about the origins of the word 'faggot', but it seems to mean 'a bundle' – as it does when applied to wood. This appears accurate, because an edible faggot is simply bits and pieces of meat held together in a bundle by a piece of caul fat (the lacy, fatty membrane surrounding the stomach and guts of the pig). These rich balls of minced meat are known as 'savoury ducks' in some areas.

Caul fat is less common that it used to be, but a traditional family butcher who knows his trade should be able to procure some for you. The fat is stiff when you buy it and needs to be soaked to make it pliable.

The best way to eat faggots is hot with 'mushy peas' and gravy made from good beef stock.

Make about 2 lb (1 kg) or 16 faggots

caul fat
1 pint (600 ml) tepid water
1 tablespoon (1 × 15 ml spoon)
   malt vinegar
1 lb (450 g) pig's liver (or a
   mixture of liver and lights)
8 oz (225 g) belly pork
2 onions

3 oz (75 g) breadcrumbs
1 egg, beaten
1 teaspoon (1 × 5 ml spoon)
   dried sage
1 teaspoon (1 × 5 ml spoon)
   dried mixed herbs
sea salt and freshly ground black
   pepper to taste

Soak the caul fat in the tepid water and vinegar until it is soft and pliable, then drain. Pre-heat the oven to gas mark 4, 350°F (180°C).

Mince the pig's liver (and lights, if using), belly pork and onions, put into a bowl and add the breadcrumbs, beaten egg, herbs and seasoning. Mix well with a fork. Divide the mixture into little balls, each weighing about 2 oz (50 g). Cut the softened caul fat into squares about 5 inches (13 cm) across, and wrap one square around each faggot.

Put the faggots into a greased baking tin so that each touches its neighbour. Bake in the oven for 30 minutes or until nicely browned on top. Remove from the oven and leave to cool, then cover the dish with aluminium foil or clingfilm and store in a cool place. Eat within 3 days.

FAGGOTS (2)

Faggots are found in many parts of Britain, and there are lots of regional variations. This Welsh version includes oatmeal instead of breadcrumbs and has different seasoning from the preceding recipe: bog myrtle was the classic herb used, although thyme is more common now. This dish is made in a big tray and the faggots are divided up part-way through the cooking.

Welsh faggots are often eaten cold with salad and apple sauce – which is not surprising when you think that the main ingredients come from a pig.

Makes about 3 lb (1.5 kg)

caul fat
1 pint (600 ml) tepid water
1 tablespoon (1 × 15 ml spoon)
  malt vinegar
2 lb (1 kg) pig's liver
2 large onions
4 oz (100 g) oatmeal
4 oz (100 g) shredded beef suet
pinch of mace

2 teaspoons (2 × 5 ml spoons)
  chopped thyme
2 teaspoons (2 × 5 ml spoons)
  sea salt
½ teaspoon (½ × 5 ml spoon)
  freshly ground black pepper

Soak the caul fat in the tepid water and vinegar until it is soft and pliable. Pre-heat the oven to gas mark 2, 300°F (150°C).

Finely mince the liver; finely chop the onions. Mix together in a large bowl and add all the remaining ingredients. Grease a large meat tin and spread the mixture evenly in the bottom. Drain the caul fat and lay it over the top. Put into the oven and cook for about 20 minutes.

Remove the tin from the oven and divide the faggot mixture into squares with a sharp knife. Return to the oven and cook for a further 20–25 minutes or until the tops of the faggots are browned. Take out of the oven and leave in the tin to cool. When cold, the faggots can be separated ready for serving. Otherwise cover the tin with aluminium foil and store in a cool place until needed. Eat within 3 days.

HASLET

Depending on where you live, this dish might be called 'haslet', 'hayslet' or 'harslet'. But whatever the pronunciation, it is first cousin to the faggot. Recipes tend to do without breadcrumbs, and there is a forthright spiciness to haslet not shared by most faggots.

Haslet is cooked whole and looks rather like a dumpy cottage loaf. It is sliced like bread and should be eaten cold; have some fiery English mustard and plenty of pickled walnuts on the table with it.

Makes about 2 lb (1 kg)

8 oz (225 g) belly pork
1 lb (450 g) pig's liver (or a
    mixture of liver and lights)
8 oz (225 g) onions
1 teaspoon (1 × 5 ml spoon)
    chopped sage

sea salt and freshly ground black
    pepper to taste
1 oz (25 g) lard

Pre-heat the oven to gas mark 5, 375°F (190°C).

Trim the belly pork, discarding any rind or bone. Chop into pieces and mince with the liver. Finely chop or mince the onions and add to meat with the sage and seasoning. (Use salt cautiously and pepper generously.)

Form the haslet into a 'cottage loaf' shape and put into a greased baking tin. Dot with lard and bake in the oven for about 30 minutes or until nicely browned on top. Remove from the oven, leave to get cold, then store in a cool place. Eat within 3 days.

STEW AND HARD

Lancastrians still rate this as one of their *real* specialities. It was once a famous pub food, eaten on Saturday nights, but is a rarity these days. The name needs some explanation: the 'stew' of the title is actually a cross between a pressed meat and a brawn, made with cheap cuts of beef and some cow heel or a pig's trotters to provide gelatinous stickiness; the 'hard' is a Lancashire oatcake, baked and then hung up to make it stiff and crisp. Put the two together and you have the perfect accompaniment to pints of North Country beer.

The oatcake recipe is on page 20.

Makes about 1 lb (450 g)

1 lb (450 g) shin of beef on the
    bone or skirt
½ cow heel or 1 pig's trotter
1 bay leaf
2 teaspoons (2 × 5 ml spoons)
    black peppercorns

1 teaspoon (1 × 5 ml spoon)
    whole allspice
1 teaspoon (1 × 5 ml spoon) sea
    salt

Trim the beef of any excess fat or gristle and steep overnight in a bowl of cold salted water, using 1 oz (25 g) salt per pint (600 ml) of water.

Drain off the salt liquid, then put the beef into a clean pan with the cleaned ½ cow heel or pig's trotter, the bay leaf and spices tied in a muslin bag and the salt. Add enough water just to cover the meat. Bring to the boil, cover with a lid and simmer over a very low heat for about 2 hours or until the beef leaves the bone and the fibres can be easily broken up. Remove the cow heel or trotter; strain off the liquor and put to one side. Then pack the beef into a dish and press down well. Return the liquor to the pan with the cow heel or pig's trotter and boil until it is concentrated and well reduced. Leave to cool, then add about 1 tablespoon (1 × 15 ml spoon) of the liquor to the beef and press again. Put a weighted board on top and leave in a cool place overnight.

The glistening jellied 'stew' can be turned out whole or spooned from the dish when ready. If covered with aluminium foil, it will keep in the larder for a couple of days.

PORK CHEESE

Butchers in Norfolk and Suffolk produce excellent versions of this East Anglian speciality, which is mid-way between brawn and potted meat. You can make it with either a fresh or pickled pork hock (a fresh hock doesn't need to be soaked).

Spread chunks of pork cheese on slices of toast and eat with mustard and pickles.

Makes about 1 lb (450 g)

1 pickled pork hock
1 teaspoon (1 × 5 ml spoon)
   ground white pepper

1 teaspoon (1 × 5 ml spoon)
   dried sage

Soak the hock in a bowl of cold water for about 12 hours, changing the water once during that time. Drain the hock, put it into a large saucepan and cover with fresh cold water. Bring to the boil, put the lid on the pan and simmer slowly until the meat leaves the bone. Lift the hock out and remove all the meat from the bones. Put the meat to one side; return the bones to the pot and continue to cook until the liquid has been reduced to about 10 fl oz (300 ml).

Mince the meat coarsely and season with pepper and sage. Strain the liquor and pour over the meat. Mix well and pack into a pot or bowl. Leave in a cool place overnight until set. The 'cheese' will keep in the larder for about 7 days if the meat has been pickled; a fresh pork cheese should be eaten within 3 days.

PRESSED SPICED PORK

This delicately spiced meat can be 'set' with gelatine, but a pig's trotter is equally effective and provides a better flavour. Serve the meat cold with sharp fruity salads.

Makes about 2 lb (1 kg)

2 lb (1 kg) hand or shoulder of pork	1 teaspoon (1 × 5 ml spoon) crushed black peppercorns
1 teaspoon (1 × 5 ml spoon) paprika	1 teaspoon (1 × 5 ml spoon) sea salt
½ teaspoon (½ × 5 ml spoon) ground cinnamon	1 pig's trotter
	2 bay leaves
½ teaspoon (½ × 5 ml spoon) ground ginger	1 pint (600 ml) pork or chicken stock

Remove the bone, fat and rind from the pork and discard. Cut the meat into 1 inch (2.5 cm) cubes. Blend together the spices and sea salt and rub well into the meat. Leave to marinate for 2 hours.

Put the pork into a saucepan with the cleaned and scrubbed trotter, bay leaves and stock. Bring to the boil, cover and simmer for about 1½ hours or until the meat is very tender. Remove the meat and set aside. Discard the trotter, then boil and reduce the liquor until about 5 fl oz (150 ml) remains.

Pack the meat into a bowl and press down well. Pour over the concentrated jellied stock. Leave to cool, then press with a weighted board for 12 hours. The spiced pork should be turned out whole and served cut into thick slices. It will keep in a cool place for 3 days.

JELLIED TONGUE

Salted or pickled pigs' tongues are best for this dish. Cure your own (see pages 34–37) or order them from the butcher. Serve cut into slices, accompanied by a sharp fruity relish such as pickled damsons.

Makes about 2 lb (1 kg)

2 lb (1 kg) pickled pigs' tongues	1 bay leaf
2 pig's trotters	1 teaspoon (1 × 5 ml spoon)
2 onions, chopped	black peppercorns
juice 1 lemon	2 slices fresh root ginger

Wash and clean the tongues and trotters and put into a pan of cold water. Bring to the boil and simmer for about 1½ hours. Remove any scum that forms and change the water half-way through the process. Then add the chopped onions and other ingredients and simmer for a further 30 minutes or until the meat is tender.

Remove the tongues and trotters from the pan, saving the cooking liquor, and leave to cool. Trim the tongues, removing the skin and any small bones and muscle from the root end. Strip the meat from the trotters. Pack the tongues and trotter meat into a bowl or dish.

Reduce the cooking liquor until it is very concentrated, strain and pour over the tongues. Leave to cool, then press under a weighted board for at least 12 hours. It will keep well for at least 7 days, particularly if the dish is covered with aluminium foil.

CHAPTER SIX

POTTING

In the summer of 1854, George Borrow embarked on a tour of Wales with his wife and daughter. After some time on the road, he found himself having breakfast at the White Lion Inn in Bala. But this was no ordinary start to the day, as he recorded in *Wild Wales* (published in 1862):

'There was tea and coffee, a goodly white loaf and butter; there were a couple of eggs and two mutton chops. There was broiled and pickled salmon – there was fried trout – there were also potted trout and potted shrimps. Mercy upon me!'

An unbeatable feast, you might think. It certainly struck a chord with Borrow and, a couple of months later, he returned to the inn, full of anticipation:

'Having dressed myself I went to the coffee-room and sat down to breakfast. What a breakfast! pot of hare; ditto of trout; pot of prepared shrimps; dish of plain shrimps; tin of sardines; beautiful beefsteak; eggs, muffin; large loaf, and butter, not forgetting capital tea. There's breakfast for you!'

Potting is one of the benchmarks of traditional British cookery, and potted foods rank with pies, pickles and hams as essentials in the larder. They found favour in the Middle Ages, when various kinds of 'cold pie' were covered and sealed not with pastry but with butter.

By Elizabethan times the technique of potting as a means of preserving all kinds of flesh had become more subtle, and more in vogue. The practice was to parboil the meat, fowl or fish, dip them in lard or clarified butter 'till they have gotten a new garment over them', pack them in stoneware pots and cover them with more butter or spiced lard. The people of Gloucester preserved Severn lampreys in this way, and there were also recipes for potting everything from swan to salmon.

The fashion for potting blossomed in the seventeenth century and these dishes graced the tables of the well-to-do; they combined the virtues of functional preserved foods with the special pleasures of the gourmet delicacy. Pigeons, woodcocks and all kinds of furred and feathered creatures found their way into pots, although Hannah Glasse's directions to 'save potted birds, that begin to be bad' must have raised a frown or two. Gradually cooks discovered that meat would keep even better if it was finely minced and beaten with butter, then pressed into pots as firmly as possible and sealed with a final layer of butter.

One of the great advantages of potting was the fact that food preserved this way would travel and keep without spoiling. It was the preferred way of preparing salmon or char for their journey from the Lake District to London, and it ensured edible provisions for voyagers on their way to Australia or the Indies. In *Food in England* (Macdonald, 1954) Dorothy Hartley recalls how one of her aunts – an early traveller to the West Indies – survived well, thanks to a fine larder stocked with hams, conserves and fruit cordials, poultry potted in tubs, salmon done in vinegar, and potted meats.

The beauty of potting is its simplicity. This sets it apart from the French tradition of pâtés and terrines. And, thanks to today's kitchen equipment, it is a very quick and easy task. Before food processors and mincers the business of potting would have occupied an entire kitchen brigade for hours on end, as they pounded flesh and ground spices.

GUIDELINES FOR POTTING

1 Choice of ingredients

Despite Hannah Glasse's comment about 'birds that begin to be bad', potting isn't a way of disguising or using up food that is almost unfit to eat. Always start with good-quality ingredients. You don't need to buy the finest cuts of meat or the most expensive fish, but the better your raw materials, the better the result. Potting is a good way of utilising cheap joints, offcuts, tail pieces of salmon and so on. In some cases you can use ready-cooked ingredients, such as beef or shrimps.

2 Preparation

Always trim away and discard any pieces of gristle, rind or bone. The ingredients need to be minced, pounded or chopped, depending on the recipe. A mincer or food processor makes the job easy.

3 Seasonings

Remember that cold food tends to have less immediate flavour than hot; the dense, pasty texture of most potted meat and fish also absorbs flavours, so use seasonings, fresh herbs and spices liberally.

4 Potting

Always press down the mixture when you put it into pots, making sure that you get rid of any pockets of air that might harbour bacteria. Leave enough head-space – say, ½ inch (1 cm) – at the top of the pot for the butter seal.

5 Clarified butter

Potted meats and fish are preserved by sealing with a layer of clarified butter. The idea of clarifying is to cleanse the butter of any foreign matter and excess salt. Even the tiniest speck of the former can hold bacteria and these can be transferred to the meat – which defeats the object of the exercise; and excess salt may spoil the seasoning of the dish, even though the butter seal isn't normally eaten. Pure fat also makes a smooth, clean-looking seal.

Melt the required amount of butter in a heavy-bottomed pan. Let it bubble for a couple of minutes, but make sure that it does not colour at all. Remove from the heat and allow to settle for 3–4 minutes, so that any particles can sink to the bottom. Do not disturb.

Once you can see a clear golden layer on top and a whitish sediment underneath, the butter can be filtered. Fold a double thickness of butter-muslin or linen over a clean bowl or jar and carefully pour the butter through it while it is still warm. The sediment will be caught by the muslin. The clarified butter can be used straight away: simply re-heat it until it bubbles, then pour carefully over the top of the mixture to be potted. If you want to store it, either cover the bowl or jar with aluminium foil, or allow the butter to harden and then form it into a cake which should also be wrapped in foil. It will keep well for weeks in a fridge or cool larder.

6 Storing

Potted meat and fish will keep for up to 1 week in a cool larder, although they are best eaten within a few days. If you use a fridge, you can store them for up to 3 weeks. The thicker the layer of butter seal, the better the pot will keep. Make sure that there are no tiny cracks in the seal. As additional protection, and to stop the butter seal shrinking, cover with an extra layer of aluminium foil – particularly if storing your potted foods in a fridge.

POTTED BEEF

There are countless recipes for potted beef: some based on raw meat, others using cooked bits and pieces; some are deliberately coarse in texture, others are smooth and pasty. Use good-quality raw beef – perhaps a piece of rump or flank – for this recipe, which produces a rough-textured dish. Also include proper beef stock – *not* made with a cube – as this gives a much fuller flavour. Eat with English mustard and assorted pickles.

Makes about 2 lb (1 kg)

2 lb (1 kg) rump or flank of beef
6 cloves
1 teaspoon (1 × 5 ml spoon) sea salt
1 teaspoon (1 × 5 ml spoon) ground white pepper
½ teaspoon (½ × 5 ml spoon) anchovy essence
10 fl oz (300 ml) warm beef stock
3 oz (75 g) clarified butter (see page 71)

Pre-heat the oven to gas mark 3, 325°F (160°C).

Trim the meat well and cut into small pieces. Pack into a deep ovenproof dish in layers, sprinkling each layer with cloves, salt, pepper and anchovy essence. Pour over the warm stock and allow it to seep through the meat. Cover the dish with aluminium foil and bake in the oven for about 2 hours or until the meat is very tender and the fibres can be broken up.

Remove the dish from the oven, take off the foil and press the meat under a weighted board until it is cold. Remove the board and cover the beef with a layer of clarified butter. Allow this to set, then store the dish in a cool place until needed. It will be good for up to 1 week.

POTTED PORK

This is a very inexpensive dish – even with the addition of wine. The pork is not pounded to a paste, but left in small chunks to give a meaty, coarse texture. Serve with a fruity accompaniment, such as Apple and Sage Jelly (prepare as for Apple and Basil Jelly on page 131).

Makes about 2 lb (1 kg)

1 lb (450 g) lean shoulder pork
1 lb (450 g) belly pork
pinch of ground mace
pinch of ground white pepper
1 teaspoon (1 × 5 ml spoon) sea
  salt

1 clove garlic, crushed
5 fl oz (150 ml) dry white wine
4 oz (100 g) clarified butter (see
  page 71)

Pre-heat the oven to gas mark 3, 325°F (160°C).

Chop the pork shoulder into small cubes. Remove any bone, rind and excess fat from the belly pork and discard, then roughly chop the meat. Mix the two lots of meat and pack into a deep ovenproof dish with the spices, salt and garlic.

Pour over the wine, cover with aluminium foil and bake in the oven for about 1½ hours. Remove the foil, then press the meat under a weighted board until cold. Take off the board and cover the potted pork with clarified butter. Allow to set, then store in a cool dry place. Eat within 1 week.

POTTED HAM WITH ROSEMARY

White Moss House, overlooking Rydal Water near Grasmere, Cumbria, started life as three eighteenth-century cottages owned by Wordsworth's family and lived in by his descendants until the 1930s. More recently the Butterworth family has transformed the place into a fine country hotel. Jean Butterworth created a kitchen devoted to the best principles of English cooking. Her son-in-law, Peter Dixon, is now chef, but the basic rules of fresh ingredients, authentic recipes and a forward-looking approach to traditional cookery are unchanged.

Potting is one of the skills of the English kitchen, and this recipe is typical of the White Moss House style.

Makes about 12 oz (350 g)

10 oz (275 g) cooked smoked ham
2 oz (50 g) butter, softened
6 fresh rosemary leaves, finely chopped

freshly ground black pepper
pinch of grated nutmeg
2 oz (50 g) clarified butter (see page 71)
slices of Ogen melon to garnish

Mince the ham twice and put it into a bowl with the softened butter. Add rosemary and season with black pepper and a little grated nutmeg. Blend well in a food processor (or pound, using a pestle and mortar).

Pack the meat into 4 individual ramekin dishes, pressing it down well to remove any air pockets. Gently melt the clarified butter and pour very carefully over the surface of the meat to seal it. Leave to cool, then store in a cool place until needed. Use within 7 days: although the ham is cured and will keep well, it is best to store the dish in the fridge if you intend keeping it any longer.

To serve, turn out each ramekin and garnish with slices of Ogen melon. Provide some wholemeal bread as well.

POTTED DUCK LIVER WITH WATER CHESTNUTS

This dish, another from Peter Dixon at White Moss House, Grasmere, is mid-way between a traditional version of potted liver and a more conventional pâté. Serve it with orange salad or Cumberland sauce.

Makes about 1½ lb (750 g)

1 onion, finely chopped
1 clove garlic, finely chopped
1 rasher lean smoked bacon, rinded and cut into small squares
1 oz (25 g) butter
1 lb (450 g) duck livers, trimmed and cleaned
2 tablespoons (2 × 15 ml spoons) brandy
juice 1 orange
1 teaspoon (1 × 5 ml spoon) Dijon mustard
1 teaspoon (1 × 5 ml spoon) ground mixed spice
sea salt and freshly ground black pepper to taste
4 oz (100 g) tinned water chestnuts, drained and chopped
4 oz (100 g) clarified butter (see page 71)

Gently fry the onion, garlic and bacon in the butter.

When the onion is translucent, add the livers and cook until sealed. Remove the onion, garlic, bacon and livers from the pan (leaving behind the juices) and liquidise; transfer to a bowl.

Add the brandy to the pan and mix well with the remaining juices. Stir in the orange juice, grated rind, mustard and mixed spice. Season with salt and pepper. Liquidise this mixture and add to the duck livers. Mix well, then add the water chestnuts and mix again. Pack into ramekin dishes, making sure that there are no air pockets.

Melt the clarified butter and pour carefully over the surface of each dish. Leave to cool and store for 24 hours in a cool place before serving.

POTTED PIGEON

Two hundred years ago, if you wanted to pot some pigeons, you would likely take a couple of dozen birds, draw them, split them open and season them with spices. Then you would pack them in a jar to mature before baking them with a lump of butter inside each bird. They were potted whole, or in halves, and were reckoned to be excellent, if eaten cold.

Nowadays we approach things differently. This dish consists of layers of pigeon meat and fat pork spiked with port and brandy. It makes an excellent first course or light lunch, served with chunks of wholemeal bread and, perhaps, some Preserved Peaches in syrup (see page 144).

Makes about 2 lb (1 kg)

3 pigeons
6 juniper berries
1 lb (450 g) belly pork
1 clove garlic, crushed
1 teaspoon (1 × 5 ml spoon)
  dried marjoram
1 teaspoon (1 × 5 ml spoon)
  freshly ground black pepper

2 tablespoons (2 × 15 ml spoons)
  port
1 tablespoon (1 × 15 ml spoon)
  brandy
4 oz (100 g) clarified butter (see
  page 71)

Clean and joint the pigeons and put them into a pan with the juniper berries. Cover with water, bring to the boil, then simmer for 20–30 minutes. Drain the pigeon joints; take the meat off the bones and cut it into strips. Put to one side.

Pre-heat the oven to gas mark 2, 300°F (150°C).

Remove any bone and rind from the pork and discard. Coarsely mince the pork with the garlic, marjoram and seasoning. Stir in the port and brandy. Put a layer of minced pork at the bottom of an ovenproof dish, then some strips of pigeon, then more pork; continue layering in this way, finishing with a full layer of pigeon. Cover the dish with aluminium foil and bake in the oven for about 1½ hours or until the meat is tender. Remove the foil and cover the dish with a layer of clarified butter. Allow to cool and set, then store until needed. It will keep for at least a week.

POTTED VENISON

This was a popular nineteenth-century delicacy, usually made with a plump shoulder of venison, which was slit in three or four places, then filled with a mixture of minced shallots, thyme, marjoram and port wine 'lees' (the sediment left after fermentation). The meat was sewn up and hung for about 9 days to 'season'. Then it was rubbed and cured with sea salt, coarse sugar, allspice and nutmeg. Finally it was baked; the lean and fat were pounded separately, seasoned with cloves, mace, cayenne and bay leaves, and packed into little pots covered with clarified butter.

A hundred years on, the recipe still holds good, although it can be simplified. It is a good way of using up offcuts from breast or shoulder of venison. Serve with brown toast and pickled damsons or Rowan Jelly (see page 133).

Makes about 2 lb (1 kg)

1½ lb (750 g) well-hung venison
8 oz (225 g) belly pork
1 clove garlic, crushed
1 teaspoon (1 × 5 ml spoon) sea
    salt
pinch of mace

pinch of freshly ground black
    pepper
1 sprig each thyme and marjoram
5 fl oz (150 ml) red wine
4 oz (100 g) clarified butter (see
    page 71)

Pre-heat the oven to gas mark 3, 325°F (160°C).

Trim the venison and pork, discarding any bone, gristle and rind. Cut the meat into small pieces. Mix with the garlic, salt and spices and pack into an ovenproof dish. Lay the sprigs of thyme and marjoram on top and pour over the red wine. Cover closely with aluminium foil and cook slowly in the oven for at least 2 hours or until the meat is very tender.

Remove the foil and herb sprigs. Then pound the meat until you have a coarse-textured mixture. Either divide into four and pack into individual pots, or press the whole mixture with a weighted board in its original dish for 2–3 hours. Cover with a layer of melted clarified butter and put in a cool place to set. This dish will keep well for up to 2 weeks if the seal is good.

POTTED SHRIMPS (1)

Morecambe Bay – that great arc of flat sands and water at the southern tip of the Lake District – has long been famous for its little brown shrimps. Even today some pub landlords, as well as fishmongers, net and pot their own catch for sale to locals and tourists. Further south there are good shrimps too. Parkgate on Merseyside, is famous, as are the large pink specimens caught off the coast of Norfolk.

Potted shrimps can be eaten as a summertime tea with brown bread and butter, or cut in slices and served with hot toast.

Makes about 1¼ lb (500 g)

1 lb (450 g) cooked fresh
  shrimps, shelled
4 oz (100 g) butter
1 teaspoon (1 × 5 ml spoon)
  ground mace

¼ teaspoon (¼ × 5 ml spoon)
  cayenne pepper
pinch of sea salt
2 oz (50 g) clarified butter (see
  page 71)

Sort through the shrimps, discarding any that are damaged or stale. Divide into 2 batches: finely chop or pound one and leave the other whole. Blend together the 2 batches in a bowl.

Melt the 4 oz (100 g) butter and add to the shrimps. Season with mace, cayenne pepper and a pinch of sea salt if necessary (boiled shrimps can be quite salty, so taste first). Blend well until the butter has been absorbed into the mixture. Press into small pots, making sure that no air pockets remain, and cover with a layer of melted clarified butter. Leave to cool, then store until needed. The shrimps will keep well for 1 week in a cool larder; for longer periods a fridge is recommended.

POTTED SHRIMPS (2)

In 1864 a certain Mr Robinson of Runcorn, 'a wholesale curer of comestibles', wrote *The Art and Mystery of Curing, Preserving and Potting (all kinds of meats, game and fish)*. It was a classic, and is still one of the few books devoted to the subject of preserving and larder foods. The selection of potting recipes, from neat's [ox] tongue and 'beef as hare' to eels and lobsters, is remarkable and the work involved in making these specialities must have been prodigious. Consider this recipe. The shrimps are prepared in the normal way, then Mr Robinson proceeds as follows:

Mix table salt ½ lb [225 g]; sifted loaf sugar ¼ lb [100 g]; cayenne pepper 1 oz [25 g]; Durham mustard [prepared from finely ground mustard seed] 1 oz [25 g].

Make four or five tablespoonfuls [4–5 × 15 ml spoons] of olive oil boiling hot in a stewpan, throw a handful of shrimps into it, and in less than a minute take them out, season them well with the mixture and lay them on dishes to cool. Continue thus to treat all the rest, and when done fill your pots and press the fish down closely. Next day cover with clarified butter, and afterwards the pots may be made secure with bladder, white or coloured paper over that. Keep them in a dry airy room. They will be much liked if taken with wine, and rectify a vitiated palate.

POTTED CRAB

The beauty of this dish is in the contrast between the fibrous white meat from the claws of the crab and the soft, pasty, 'brown' meat from the body. Cayenne pepper is a vital ingredient and should be used fearlessly.

Makes about 1 lb (450 g)

1 large boiled crab or 12 oz (350 g) dressed crabmeat (including both white and dark meat)
pinch of freshly ground black pepper
pinch of ground mace
½ teaspoon (½ × 5 ml spoon) cayenne pepper, or to taste

squeeze of lemon juice
pinch of sea salt
6 oz (175 g) butter
3 oz (75 g) clarified butter (see page 71)

If using a whole crab, remove the 'dead men's fingers' and other inedible bits, and discard. (If you are unsure about how to do this, ask the fishmonger to do it for you.) Pick all the flesh out of the shell, keeping the white meat and the creamy dark meat separate.

Season the crabmeat with the spices, lemon juice and a little salt; taste and adjust if necessary. Then pack firmly into 1 large round pot, or 4 small ones, arranging the white and dark meat in alternate layers. Melt the 6 oz (175 g) butter and pour it over the crab, so that it is just covered.

Leave in a cool place, then cover with a layer of melted clarified butter to seal. Store in a cool dry place and eat within 1 week.

POTTED CHAR

Char are the least known and least common members of the salmon family. In the British Isles they are confined to deep inland lakes – especially Lake Windermere in Cumbria. *Salvelinus willughbii*, the Windermere char, is a handsome creature rather like a trout, with a dark greenish-brown back fading to silver and an orange or sometimes deep red belly.

Potted char became popular in the second half of the eighteenth century when the Lake District experienced its first tourist explosion. In addition to the recipe itself, visitors were intrigued by the distinctive hand-painted char pots used for the finished dish. Freelance journeyman decorators created the artwork for these shallow containers and, in time, they became fashionable *objets d'art*. In 1759, when Elizabeth Raffald's recipe for potted char appeared in print (in *The Experienced English Housekeeper*), these 'broad, thin pots' were already well known to English cooks. Here is her recipe:

> Cut off the fins, and cheek-part of each side of the head of your chars, rip them open, take out the guts and the blood from the backbone, dry them well in a cloth, lay them on a board, and throw on them a good deal of salt, let them stand all night, then scrape it gently off them, and wipe them exceedingly well with a cloth, pound mace, cloves, and nutmeg, very fine, throw a little on the inside of them, and a good deal of salt and pepper on the outside, put them close down in a deep pot, with their bellies up, with plenty of clarified butter over them, set them in the oven, and let them stand for three

hours; when they come out, pour what butter you can off clear, lay a board over them, and turn them upside down, to let the gravy run from them, scrape the salt and pepper very carefully off, and season them exceeding well both inside and out with the above seasoning, lay them close in broad thin pots for that purpose, with their backs up, then cover them well with clarified butter; keep them in a cool dry place.

In recent times the uncrowned queen of potted char was the late Bronwen Nixon, the guiding spirit behind Rothay Manor, an enchanting Regency hotel tucked away in one of the backwaters of Ambleside. This is an adapted version of the recipe used in her kitchen. If you cannot procure char, trout is an economical alternative; offcuts and tail pieces of salmon and salmon trout can also be substituted.

Makes about 1½ lb (750 g)

4 char, each weighing about 6 oz
  (175 g)
5 fl oz (150 ml) dry white wine
1 bay leaf
1 strip lemon peel
pinch of ground mace

4 oz (100 g) butter
squeeze of lemon juice
sea salt and freshly ground black
  pepper to taste
3 oz (75 g) clarified butter (see
  page 71)

Pre-heat the oven to gas mark 2, 300°F (150°C).

Clean the fish and pack them closely in a shallow ovenproof dish. Add the wine, bay leaf, lemon peel and mace. Dot with 1 oz (25 g) of the butter and bake in the oven for about 30 minutes or until tender. Drain the fish, reserving the cooking liquor, and discard the head, tail and bones.

Strain the cooking liquor, then reduce it over a high heat until it is very concentrated. Add the remaining 3 oz (75 g) butter and stir until it is melted. Flake the fish and blend it in a food processor with the buttery cooking liquor and lemon juice. Season to taste with salt and pepper.

Pack into small pots, press down and leave to cool. Pour on a layer of melted clarified butter and allow to set. Store for at least 24 hours and eat within 2 days.

CHAPTER SEVEN

RAISED PIES AND PASTIES

It's easy to see why pies have been so popular for more than 2000 years. They are convenient and versatile; they can be functional or ceremonial; they can serve as nutritious food for working people or festive centrepieces for great occasions. The tradition of the savoury pie is part of the legacy of British cookery and even the earliest printed recipes included instructions for 'pyes' in 'coffynes of pastrye'.

These pies of the past were usually 'raised' by making a case (or 'coffyne') of pastry and filling it with all kinds of tit-bits, richly spiced and often including plenty of dried fruit. They were monumental, elaborately decorated and given pride of place at table. Cut one open and you would find an extraordinary collection of sweet and savoury morsels, including fish as well as meat or game. Batalia Pye, one of the great seventeenth-century recipes, required 4 game pigeons, 4 ox 'palates', 6 lambs' 'stones' (testicles), 6 veal sweetbreads, 20 cockscombs, 4 artichoke bottoms, 1 pint (600 ml) oysters, the marrow of 3 bones, butter, gravy, lemons, mace and seasoning.

The range of pies was enormous until the beginning of the nineteenth century when potatoes started to supersede pastry as the staple, filling accompaniment to meat or fish. There were mince pies made with meat or fruit; others filled with pickled herrings, pears and currants; there were meatless pies for Lent and some made as royal tributes: the Gloucester Pie, offered to sovereigns from Richard III to Queen Victoria, was a 20 lb (9 kg) monster containing lampreys from the River Severn, crayfish and truffles and was decorated with a crown and sceptre.

Raised pies had several advantages. They could be eaten cold with the fingers – in the days before knives and forks were common on the table – they would keep well, and the heavy pastry case could withstand long bumpy journeys. This led to some gargantuan feats of culinary construction, worthy of any *Guinness Book of Records*. On 6 January 1770 *The Newcastle Chronicle* reported the following incident:

> Monday last was brought from Howick to Berwick, to be shipp'd to London, for Sir Hen. Grey, a pie, the contents thereof are as follows: viz. 2 bushels of flour, 20 lbs of butter, 4 geese, 2 turkies, 2 rabbits, 4 wild ducks, 2 woodcocks, 6 snipes and 4 partridges; 2 neats' tongues, 2 curlews, 7 blackbirds, and 6 pigeons; it is supposed a very great curiosity, was made by Mrs Dorothy Patterson, housekeeper at Howick. It was near nine feet in circumference at the bottom, weighs about twelve stones, will take two men to present it to table; it is neatly fitted with a case, and four small wheels to facilitate its use to every guest that inclines to partake of its contents at table.
>
> (Quoted in *The Cookery of England* by Elisabeth Ayrton, Andre Deutsch, 1974.)

In Yorkshire cooks created equally spectacular pies for Christmas feasting. Surrounded by a heavy pastry case there would be a turkey stuffed with a goose, a chicken, a partridge and a pigeon, all boned and fitted one inside the other. In the spaces there would be hare, woodcock and wild fowl, plus about 4 lb (1.75 kg) butter to seal everything together. Sadly the pies of the past now seem inconvenient, impractical, ludicrously expensive and somehow irrelevant. Pastry's reputation as a heavy fattening food has meant that pies are often eaten hot, for their filling alone. The great tradition has been whittled away. We now seem content with factory-made pork pies of dubious quality, perhaps a slice or two of veal and ham pie with egg, and a piece of game pie as a Christmas treat.

Most commercially produced pies are dreadful. A run-of-the-mill pork pie, for example, can contain as little as 25 per cent 'meat' (and that is taken to include fat, skin, gristle and much more, as well as genuine lean meat). The filling is likely to include flavour enhancers, preservatives, sometimes polyphosphates and colouring as well. Fat is cheap, so both the filling and the pastry will be loaded with it. If there is any jelly, it will be a meagre amount of artificial stuff tasting of nothing. However, there are still bakers and pie-makers who know their trade, who take care with ingredients and cherish their craft. Home cooks should follow their example.

GUIDELINES FOR MAKING RAISED PIES AND PASTIES

Pie-making isn't difficult, but it takes time and you need to be organised. As a rule, prepare the jellied stock first, then the filling and finally the pastry.

1   The jellied stock

Many pies – especially the raised kind – need good jelly. You can make this using gelatine, but much better results can be obtained from a proper stock, prepared from bones and reduced by boiling until it is very concentrated. Use bones from the same meat as the filling: for example, pork bones to make stock for pork pies, game carcases for game pies and so on.

assorted bones	2 teaspoons (2 × 5 ml spoons)
1–2 pig's trotters	black peppercorns
1 onion, chopped	1 bunch fresh herbs
2 carrots, chopped	pinch of sea salt (optional)

Put the bones and cleaned trotter(s) in a saucepan with the onion, carrots and peppercorns. Cover with water. Bring to the boil, then simmer for at least 2–3 hours (the longer the better). Strain off the stock, put into another pan and boil hard until it is reduced to about 10–15 fl oz (300–450 ml). Taste and add a little salt if necessary. Leave to cool. The stock will keep well for a couple of days, if covered and left in a cool place. Once it has set it will need to be slightly warmed so that it can be poured easily into the pie. Normally the jellied stock is added as soon as the pie comes out of the oven, so that the juices can seep into the pastry. Use a funnel for pouring and work very slowly, otherwise you will flood the pie.

2   The filling

Always use good-quality ingredients, in particular naturally reared or organic pork or beef. Well-trimmed lean meat is essential, but raised pies and pasties also need a decent proportion of fat to keep them moist and succulent. For most recipes fine chopping, rather than mincing, is the best method of handling the meat. Use plenty of spices and seasoning, particularly if the pie is to be eaten cold.

3   The pastry

Most pies and pasties for keeping are made with shortcrust or hot-water pastry. Successful pastry depends on good baking, so make sure that the oven is pre-heated to the correct temperature before you begin. If the temperature is too low, the pastry will sink and become heavy; if it is too high, the outside will burn and the inside will remain uncooked. Always make pastry in a cool place.

Shortcrust pastry

A very versatile, rich pastry, ideal for pasties that are to be eaten cold.

Makes about 1½ lb (675 g)

1 lb (450 g) plain flour   8 oz (225 g) butter or margarine
pinch of sea salt   5 fl oz (150 ml) very cold water

Sift the flour and salt together. Chop the butter or margarine into pieces and rub into the flour with your fingers until the mixture looks like fine breadcrumbs and there is no unblended flour clinging to the sides of the bowl. Add very cold water slowly and carefully until you have a soft dough which will roll easily but is not at all sticky. Form into a ball. Roll out the pastry quite thickly, otherwise it will be unworkable. Shortcrust pastry will keep for several days if wrapped in greaseproof paper and stored in a cool place.

Hot-water pastry

The classic pastry for hand-raised pies.

Makes about 1½ lb (675 g)

1 lb (450 g) plain flour   6 oz (175 g) lard
½ teaspoon (½ × 5 ml spoon) sea   5 fl oz (150 ml) water
   salt

Sift the flour and salt in a bowl and make a well in the middle. Put the lard in a saucepan wih the water, bring to the boil and pour immediately over the flour. Turn and mix well with a wooden spoon until you have a ball of soft dough. Cover and leave for about 10 minutes so that the dough can cool off a little. While the dough is still warm, but not too hot to handle, cut off and set aside about one quarter for the pie lid.

There are two methods of raising the pastry. If you are using a cake tin with a removable base or a hinged pie mould, put the dough at the bottom and gradually work it up the sides with your fingers, turning the base if necessary. Make sure that there are no cracks, otherwise the pie juices will leak out. If the pastry doesn't stand up, it is too hot: wait for a few minutes, then start again. Once the pastry is up to the top of the mould, you can pack in the filling, making sure that the meat fills the corners and any crevices of the mould.

Alternatively you can raise the pastry around the outside of a special wooden pie mould or even a jam jar. Flour the mould before you start, otherwise the pastry will stick. Place the mould in the centre of the lump of pastry and gradually raise it up the sides, flouring your fingers as you proceed. This needs a little practice, but it's worth the effort, because the resulting pastry is light and crisp. Leave the pastry to cool and 'set'. (If you wish, you can tie a piece of thick paper around the outside so that the pastry retains its shape.) Carefully remove the mould and add the filling to the pastry case.

To make the lid, roll out the reserved piece of pastry, trim it and fit it on top of the pie, moistening the edges with milk and crimping them together with your forefinger and thumb.

MELTON MOWBRAY PORK PIE

The classic hand-raised pork pie is traditionally associated with the town of Melton Mowbray in Leicestershire. This is the home of the pie-maker's craft and it has produced more than its share of local mythology and folk-lore. Treatises have been written about the Melton pie industry, disputes about recipes have featured in the press and giant pies have been presented to English football clubs.

Melton may be the eponymous centre of the trade, but excellent pies of similar character are still made in many parts of the country, although the strongholds are in Nottinghamshire, Lincolnshire and Derbyshire, as well as Leicestershire. Recipes vary from place to place: some include anchovy essence, others may have a little chopped apple in the filling, and each pie boasts its own individual seasoning.

Apart from the skill involved in making hot-water pastry, good pork pies depend on good-quality meat, which should be chopped rather than minced and should contain enough fat to keep the filling moist (aim for about two parts lean to one part fat).

Makes 1 large or 2 medium pies

2 lb (1 kg) hand or shoulder of pork
1 teaspoon (1 × 5 ml spoon) chopped fresh sage
½ teaspoon (½ × 5 ml spoon) ground allspice
sea salt and freshly ground black pepper to taste

1 lb (450 g) hot-water pastry (see page 85)
1 egg, beaten
a little milk
10 fl oz (300 ml) concentrated jellied stock (see page 84)

Trim the meat, discarding any bones and rind, and chop finely. Mix with the chopped sage, allspice and seasoning. (You can test the seasoning by frying a small portion of the mixture, tasting it and adjusting if necessary.)

Make the pastry. Keep a portion to one side for the lid(s) and raise the remainder into 1 or 2 moulds (see pages 85–6), depending on your needs. Make the pie lid(s) with the reserved pastry. Pre-heat the oven to gas mark 6, 400°F (200°C).

When the pastry is cool, pack the meat carefully into the pie case(s) so that all corners and crevices are filled. Brush the rim of the pie(s) with milk and fit on the lid(s). Make a hole in the top and glaze with beaten egg.

Put the pie(s) on a greased baking tray and cook in the oven for 30 minutes. Then reduce the oven temperature to gas mark 3, 325°F (160°C), and bake for a further 60 minutes (add an extra 20 minutes if you are cooking 1 large pie instead of 2 medium ones). Remove the pie(s) from the oven and immediately pour the jellied stock through the hole in the lid(s). Leave in a cool place to set. Pork pies should be eaten within 2 days – in fact, they are at their best a few hours after baking.

GAME PIE

A favourite raised pie for the Christmas festivities. Make it with any assortment of game that you can lay your hands on – pheasant, venison, pigeon, wild rabbit, hare – and use the bones to make the stock for the pie.

Makes 1 large pie

8 oz (225 g) belly pork
4 rashers streaky bacon
½ teaspoon (½ × 5 ml spoon) each grated nutmeg, ground cinnamon and ground cloves
sea salt and freshly ground black pepper
1 lb (450 g) game meat (boned weight)
3 tablespoons (3 × 15 ml spoons) brandy

1 tablespoon (1 × 15 ml spoon) chopped parsley
1 lb (450 g) hot-water pastry (see page 85)
a little milk
1 egg, beaten
1 pint (600 ml) game stock (made from bones: see page 84)

Trim the pork and bacon, discarding any bone and rind. Mince together and season with the spices, salt and pepper. Chop the game into neat little pieces (mince any ragged trimmings and add to the pork). Put the game meat into a dish with the brandy and marinate for 2 hours.

Prepare the hot-water pastry and set aside a quarter for the pie lid. Form the rest into a mould (see pages 85–6). Make the pie lid. Pre-heat the oven to gas mark 6, 400°F (200°C).

When the pie case is cool, pack it with layers of pork and game, beginning and ending with pork. (Any liquor from the game marinade can be included in the pie.) Brush the edges of the pie case with milk and fit on the lid. Crimp the edges together and make a hole in the top. Brush with beaten egg and bake in the oven for 30 minutes. Reduce the oven temperature to gas mark 3, 325°F (160°C), and cook for a further 45–60 minutes depending on the thickness and density of the pie.

Meanwhile, in a pan on top of the stove, reduce the stock until you have about 10 fl oz (300 ml), then let it cool. As soon as the pie comes out of the oven, carefully pour the stock through the hole in the lid. Leave in a cool place to set. The pie should keep well for at least 7 days.

BEEF AND EGG PIE

An interesting West Country variation, using beef instead of the more usual pork or veal and ham. This sturdy raised pie is best eaten cold with mustard and pickles.

Makes 1 large or 2 medium pies

1 lb (450 g) chuck steak
2 oz (50 g) shredded beef suet
1 teaspoon (1 × 5 ml spoon) sea salt
1 teaspoon (1 × 5 ml spoon) ground white pepper
2 hard-boiled eggs

12 oz (375 g) hot-water pastry (see page 85)
a little milk
1 egg, beaten
5 fl oz (150 ml) jellied beef stock (see page 84)

Trim the meat, discarding any fat or gristle, and mince finely. Add the shredded suet and seasoning. Prepare the pastry, set aside a quarter for the lid(s) and raise the rest into 1 large or 2 medium-sized moulds (see pages 85–6). Make the pie lid(s). Pre-heat the oven to gas mark 7, 425°F (220°C).

When the pastry is cool, pack the filling into the case(s) and press the whole hard-boiled eggs into the middle of the mixture. Brush the edges of the pastry case(s) with milk and fit on the lid(s). Make a hole in the centre of the lid(s) and brush with beaten egg.

Put the pie(s) on to a greased baking tray and cook in the oven for 20 minutes. Then reduce the temperature to gas mark 3, 325°F (160°C), and bake for a further 45 minutes or until the pastry is browned and the filling well cooked. Remove from the oven and allow to cool.

Meanwhile, boil the stock until it is sticky and concentrated. Let it cool, then pour a little through the hole in the lid of the pie(s). Leave in a cool place so that the jelly can set. Eat within 3 days.

MUTTON PIES

'Fine mutton pies, fat piping hot; One for a penny, two for a groat.' Glaswegians used to call these little pies 'tuppenny struggles' and, as the rhyme suggests, they were eaten 'piping hot' – although they were equally popular served cold with pickled red cabbage.

Makes 4 pies

1 lb (450 g) lean mutton or mature lamb (leg or shoulder)
1 onion, chopped
1 teaspoon (1 × 5 ml spoon) Worcestershire sauce or mushroom ketchup
½ teaspoon (½ × 5 ml spoon) ground mace

4 tablespoons (4 × 15 ml spoons) beef or lamb stock
12 oz (375 g) hot-water pastry (see page 85)
1 egg, beaten

Trim the meat, discarding any fat, gristle and bone, then mince or chop finely. Blend with the chopped onion, sauce or ketchup and seasoning, then add sufficient stock to moisten the mixture.

Prepare the pastry, pat into a flat shape and divide into 4 equal pieces. Mould each piece into a pie case about 3 inches (7.5 cm) high. Use the trimmings to form the lids. Pre-heat the oven to gas mark 2, 300°F (150°C).

When the pastry is cool, pack each mould with a portion of the filling, dampen the edges and pinch on the lid. Make a slit in the top of each pie and brush with beaten egg. Put on to a baking tray and cook in the oven for about 45 minutes or until the filling is cooked through.

Eat straight away, or leave on a wire rack to cool. The pies will keep for a couple of days if stored in a cool place.

CUMBERLAND PIE

Mince pies originally contained meat and this regional recipe is typical of the kind of dish produced in large quantities for keeping during the winter months. Rum was a favourite ingredient of many Lakeland specialities.

Makes 2 large pies

1½ lb (750 g) lean lamb or mutton
1 lb (450 g) raisins
8 oz (225 g) currants
4 oz (100 g) candied peel
pinch of grated nutmeg
pinch of ground mixed spice
1 lb (450 g) soft brown sugar

sea salt and ground white pepper to taste
4 fl oz (120 ml) dark rum
2 lb (1 kg) hot-water pastry (see page 85)
a little milk
1 egg, beaten

Trim the meat, discarding any fat or gristle, and mince well. Chop or mince the dried fruit and add to the meat along with the spices, sugar and seasoning. Moisten with rum and leave overnight.

Prepare the pastry and divide in half. Use each piece to line an oval pie mould, putting aside enough for the lids. Make the lids from the reserved pastry. Pre-heat the oven to gas mark 7, 425°F (220°C).

When the pastry cases are full, fill with the meat mixture, moisten the edges with milk and fit on the lids. Make a hole in the top of each and brush with beaten egg. Bake in the oven for 30 minutes, then reduce the temperature to gas mark 3, 325°F (160°C), and cook for a further 1½ hours or until thoroughly browned. Remove from the oven and eat hot or cold. The pies will keep well for at least a week in the larder.

DEVIZES PIE

Traditions live on in unlikely places. Devizes Pie – a pie by name, but not by nature – was thought by many to be extinct, yet if you pay a visit to the Bear Hotel in Devizes, Wiltshire, you will find it on the menu. The recipe was discovered in *The Magazine of Domestic Economy* (1836) by Florence White, who founded the English Folk Cookery Association in the 1930s.

Devizes Pie is an elaborate brawn cooked under a pastry crust. When it is cooked, the pastry is removed, the contents are allowed to set and then served in slices with pickled eggs and mustard. The original recipe uses a calf's head, but half a pig's head is safer and more practical these days.

Makes 1 large pie

½ pig's head
2 onions, chopped
2 carrots, chopped
1 turnip, chopped
1 bunch mixed fresh herbs
sea salt and freshly ground black
  pepper to taste
4 oz (100 g) lean lamb (leg or
  shoulder)
4 oz (100 g) unsmoked bacon

6 oz (175 g) pickled tongue
4 hard-boiled eggs, sliced
½ teaspoon (½ × 5 ml spoon)
  cayenne pepper
1 teaspoon (1 × 5 ml spoon)
  ground allspice
8 oz (225 g) hot-water pastry (see
  page 85)
parsley and pickled eggs to
  garnish

Get the butcher to clean and prepare the head. Scrub thoroughly and blanch in boiling water. Drain and put into a large pan with the chopped onions, carrots and turnip, the herbs and a little seasoning. Cover with water and simmer for about 2 hours or until the meat falls from the bone. Take the head out of the pan and set aside. Strain the stock, boil until it is reduced to about 10 fl oz (300 ml) and set this aside also.

Remove the meat from the head and cut into thin slices. Finely chop the lamb and bacon and cut the tongue into strips. Pack all the meat into a pie dish with the hard-boiled egg slices, arranging decoratively in layers and sprinkling with cayenne and allspice. Pour in enough jellied stock to surround the meat. Pre-heat the oven to gas mark 3, 325°F (160°C).

Prepare the pastry and use to cover the meat. Make a slit in the top of the pastry lid. Bake in the oven for about 1½ hours. Remove the pie from the oven, allow to cool, then remove the pastry lid. Turn out the filling on to a dish and serve garnished with parsley and sliced pickled eggs.

CORNISH PASTIES

What goes into a Cornish pasty? There's an old Cornish rhyme that spells it out:

> Pastry rolled out like a plate,
> Piled with turmut, tates and mate,
> Doubled up and baked like fate,
> That's a Cornish pasty.

'Turmut, tates and mate' (turnips, potatoes and meat) form the classic filling, although the recipe has been abused by manufacturers – as anyone who has visited a café or railway station buffet will know. Today the traditional mixture of a good Cornish pasty usually includes onion as well, but the unique flavour of the real thing still derives from the fact that the raw meat is actually cooked inside the pastry case.

The size and shape also vary. Torpedoes, with the pastry seam at the top are most common nowadays, although in Cornwall they still fold the pastry over to make something much flatter. Pasties are the perfect portable meal, an edible lunch box with all the ingredients packed inside. Farm labourers, fishermen and tin miners all survived on them and they were often marked at one corner with the owner's initials so that each man's pasty was easily identifiable – even when it was half-eaten.

Naturally pasty recipes provoke intense partisan loyalties. This version comes from the Cornish Women's Institute. To produce the right flavour and texture, the shortcrust pastry should be made with lard rather than butter or margarine.

Makes 2 large pasties

8 oz (225 g) shortcrust pastry (see page 85)
2 large potatoes, thinly sliced
2 small turnips, thinly sliced
2 medium onions, chopped
8 oz (225 g) lean beef (skirt or chuck steak), finely chopped
sea salt and freshly ground black pepper
1 oz (225 g) beef dripping (optional)
a little milk

Prepare the pastry. Pre-heat the oven to gas mark 6, 400°F (200°C).
    Divide the pastry in half and roll out into 2 rounds. Arrange some

potato on half of each round. Season, then add a thin layer of turnip and a layer of onion. Season again, then add the meat. Dot with a knob or two or dripping, if you wish. Then cover with another layer of potato.

Dampen the edges of the pastry and fold over. Press the edges together firmly and crimp them. Brush with milk and make a slit in the centre for the steam to escape. Bake in the oven for 20 minutes, then reduce the temperature to gas mark 4, 350°F (180°C), and cook for a further 40 minutes or until golden brown. Eat hot or cold.

VENISON PASTIES

These rich pasties are quick and easy to make. Ideally use meat from haunch or saddle of venison, but cheaper cuts will suffice. Excellent cold with Rowan Jelly (see page 133).

Makes 2 large or 4 small pasties

1 lb (450 g) venison
2 onions, finely chopped
1 pint (600 ml) beef stock
10 fl oz (300 ml) red wine
2 teaspoons (2 × 5 ml spoons) redcurrant jelly
sea salt and freshly ground black pepper to taste

2 teaspoons (2 × 5 ml spoons) mixed chopped parsley and marjoram
1 lb (450 g) shortcrust pastry (see page 85)
a little milk
1 egg, beaten

Trim the venison, discarding any fat, sinew or gristle, and cut into small cubes. Put into a saucepan with the onions and stock. Bring to the boil, then pour in the red wine and add the redcurrant jelly, salt and pepper. Reduce the heat, cover and simmer for about 40 minutes or until the meat is very tender. Strain the meat, reserving the stock, and set both aside to cool.

Pre-heat the oven to gas mark 4, 350°F (180°C). Prepare the pastry, roll out and divide into 2 large (or 4 small) oblongs. Place a portion of the meat in the centre of each piece, sprinkle with some chopped herbs and fold the pastry over. Brush the edges with a little milk, then crimp them together. Make a slit near the top and brush with beaten egg. Put the pasties on a greased baking tray and cook in the oven for about 20 minutes for large pasties, 10–15 minutes for small ones.

Meanwhile, reduce the stock until it is quite concentrated. Remove the pasties from the oven, enlarge the slit in each one and pour in a little of the stock. Leave in a cool place to get cold.

FORFAR BRIDIES

In their original form, bridies were made with the best steak which was cooked quickly and wrapped in a simple flour-and-water paste. These days they are more like a Scottish version of the Cornish pasty.

Makes 4 bridies

1 lb (450 g) topside or rump
  steak
3 oz (75 g) shredded beef suet
2 oz (50 g) onions, chopped
5 fl oz (150 ml) beef stock
sea salt and freshly ground black
  pepper to taste

1 lb (450 g) shortcrust pastry (see
  page 85)
a little milk
1 egg, beaten

Pre-heat the oven to gas mark 4, 350°F (180°C).

Trim the meat, discarding any fat or gristle, and cut into thin strips. Mix with the suet, onions, a little stock and seasoning.

Prepare the pastry, roll it out and cut into 4 ovals. Cover half of each oval with a portion of meat and fold over the other half to make a crescent or half-moon shape. Moisten the edges with milk and crimp together. Brush with beaten egg and make a little hole at the top of each bridie for steam to escape. Put on to a greased baking tray and cook in the oven for about 45 minutes or until golden brown.

CHAPTER EIGHT

SMOKED FISH

Fish smoking is an ancient craft. It began as a chance discovery some time in prehistory, when tribes of nomadic hunter-gatherers roamed across the land in search of food. They visited the seas and rivers for fish, but they had to find some way of preserving their seasonal harvests. The obvious idea was to hang up the day's catch in the salty air to dry. It wasn't long before they noticed that fish suspended over the smoke of their fires kept even better *and* had a distinctive, rather appealing flavour.

Smoked fish are one of the great glories of the British larder, and over the centuries curers have devised scores of classic specialities: first there were heavily cured red herrings, 'kippered' salmon and sprats; later came bloaters, kippers themselves, eel, Finnan haddock, Arbroath smokies and many more. But tastes have changed, and so have curing processes. The strong flavours of the past, generated out of food preservation as a necessity, have been replaced by something much milder and more subtle.

Technology has changed too. In the past fish was smoked over smouldering fires, either in cottage chimneys or in specially constructed brick smokehouses, filled with row upon row of fish hung on poles or rods. Curers needed a workforce of men simply to climb into these places, moving the rows of fish around to obtain an even cure and counteract any unpredictable changes in the wind which caused the smoke to blow in the wrong direction. Traditional smokehouses like this are still used by some curers today, and they produce excellent results if well managed. Not surprisingly, however, other methods have been devised to speed up and standardise the process and make it more controlled. The Torry kiln, developed in 1939 by the Ministry of Agriculture at the Torry Research

Station in Aberdeen, is the best-known. This mechanical kiln can smoke large quantities of fish in a few hours, it cuts down on wastage, there is less work involved and the results are consistent. Certainly fish smoked by these methods may be consistent, but it is often consistently mediocre. Flavours are dull and predictable, without the individual character or the real class of the best examples from traditional smokehouses.

Food technologists have even tried to do away with real smoke altogether, by dipping the fish into a tank of 'liquid smoke' or spraying it with a smoke-flavoured solution. Thankfully these methods have made little headway, and many of the chemicals have subsequently been outlawed. The other contentious issue surrounding smoked fish is the use of dyes, though this is nothing new. Cochineal was used in the eighteenth century to colour sprats, salt fish were often washed in water to which lichen had been added to produce a yellow colour, and the orange-yellow dye annato (derived from the seeds of the tropical plant *Bixa orellana*) has been used on smoked cod and haddock for many years.

'There are manufacturers who injure the smoking business by manufacturing smoked herring which have not been near smoke by curing the herring with a specially prepared yellowish brown varnish or oil which imparts to the herring a little of a smoky flavour.' This complaint comes from an American report published in 1884. The implications are obvious, and even more serious in our own time. Dyes and smoke-flavoured chemicals can be – and have been – used to deceive the public. Brown FK and tartrazine have been widely employed by commercial curers for kippers and smoked haddock respectively. For a long time they believed that consumers wanted fish with an intense, unnatural colour. But attitudes are changing. Concern and public awareness about additives and their potential dangers have forced some curers to do away with their dyes and go back to producing smoked fish without chemical 'pit props' or cosmetic tricks. And if you want to smoke your own, there is no need to consider these substances at all.

GUIDELINES FOR SMOKING FISH

With space, time and reliable supplies of fresh fish, you can try some small-scale smoking. However, if you are a beginner, don't undertake anything too ambitious until you have had some practice and understand the finer points of the process. Start with a few sprats of herring before moving on to more expensive items such as salmon. Also enlist help from someone who knows the trade while you are still learning.

1 Equipment

The essential piece of equipment for fish smoking is some kind of smokehouse or smoking apparatus. Basically you need a smoking chamber, a source of smoke and some way of controlling draughts. You can adapt an old brick outhouse into a smokehouse, convert a defunct cooker, or invent some apparatus made of wood and metal. It requires a mixture of engineering talent and ingenuity.

The simplest device is a barrel smoker. Obtain an old wooden beer cask and knock out both ends. You will also need: bricks to raise the barrel off the ground – these can be adjusted to control the draught and provide access to the fire; a damp sack to put over the top of the barrel during smoking to concentrate the dense smoke inside; and a thin rectangular metal sheet, which is placed on the bricks and should be narrower in width than the barrel to allow air and smoke to rise (such a sheet can be improvised from the top of a large biscuit tin).

You will also need a selection of metal rods, stout lengths of wire, hooks and twine – all for suspending the fish across the top of the barrel. A wire rack is useful if you wish to smoke fillets or chunks of fish. A supply of sawdust and chippings can be obtained from a local carpenter, sawmill or wood yard (check the telephone directory or local newspaper for details).

Other requirements are a white plastic bucket or large bowl for brining, some wooden spoons and tongs, good sharp kitchen knives, a chopping board and other standard kitchen equipment for cleaning, filleting and preparing the fish.

2 Preparing the fish

Always use fresh fish for smoking. Don't be tempted to cut corners – or costs – by purchasing poor-quality fish or anything that is past its best. There are several classic signs of freshness: bright eyes, firm springy flesh and a glistening lustre on the skin and scales. Fresh fish should have very little smell – apart from a hint of the sea.

The fish may be left whole, gutted or otherwise, or be split or filleted before curing, depending on the product.

3   Salting and brining

Fish needs to be salted or brined before being smoked. This tones up the flesh, adds flavour and helps in preservation. Brine is used for most types of smoked fish, although salmon is generally dry-salted. Salt also helps to produce a gloss or 'pellicle' on the surface of the fish once it is in the smokehouse.

To make a brine, dissolve 2½ lb (1.25 kg) rock or sea salt in 8 pints (4.5 litres) water in a suitable container, such as a plastic bucket. You may need to heat the water to ensure that all the salt dissolves. Then leave it until completely cold before putting in any fish. Brining time depends on the type of fish and the style of cure, but large thick specimens will need longer than small ones. Keep the fish submerged by putting on top of them a piece of wood that you have washed thoroughly in boiling water.

For dry-salting, it is best to use sea salt because of its superior flavour. Sprinkle a layer of salt over the bottom of a large stainless-steel dish or tray, put the fish on top, then cover with another layer of salt and any other seasonings of your choice. Dry-salting takes longer than brining, and the time needed depends largely on the thickness of the fish.

4   Drying

After salting, the fish is hung up to dry. Whole fish are strung on 'speats' (rods), which are threaded through the eye sockets or through the gills and mouth. Split fish, such as kippers, are pinned up on 'tenterhooks' stuck through the thick shoulder flesh. Fillets are draped over frames, while small items or chunks of fish are usually laid on racks. Drying can take several hours.

5   Wood and smoke

Smoke gives flavour and colour, it has some preservative effect and provides a protective film on the surface of the fish. Wood smoke consists of vapours and minute droplets containing a large number of different compounds including phenols, acids, lactones, carbonyl compounds, alcohols and esters. The phenols seem to be particularly important, because they produce much of the characteristic 'smoky' flavour and have an antioxidant and bactericidal effect – in other words, they stop fat turning rancid and destroy bacteria which might cause the fish to decay.

The traditional way of producing smoke is to burn sawdust or wood chippings slowly. It is important to let the fire smoulder, so that it produces a great deal of smoke but very little flame. As a rule, hardwoods are best for smoking; softwoods from coniferous trees contain resins which produce an unpleasant bitter flavour and may give the fish a dark tarry appearance.

The choice of wood depends on geography, local distribution and what is available – although a strong tradition has grown up over the years. In England oak, beech, elm and ash are popular; Scotland has birch and aromatic juniper wood; Ireland's peat was often used in place of wood, while in North America the range includes hickory, scrub oak, apple wood, orange and sweet bay, as well as coconut husks and corn cobs.

6 Cold- and hot-smoking

There are two distinct methods of smoking fish. Cold-smoking refers to the temperature of the smoke, which should not rise above 85°F (30°C). The flesh of the fish remains 'raw', but it is impregnated with smoke, and is also partially dried during the process. Most British smoked fish are cold-smoked: for example, kippers, bloaters, Finnan haddock, salmon and some mackerel, as well as more exotic items including monkfish and halibut.

In hot-smoking the temperature can rise to 250°F (120°C), although about 180°F (82°C) is more common. The fish is actually cooked during the smoking, as well as being flavoured and preserved. This is the basic method for trout, Arbroath smokies, eel, buckling (hot-smoked herring) and most European smoked fish.

7 The smoking process

The actual smoking process is quite straightforward, although it needs a fair amount of practice. Once the fish have been dried, put the rods or racks across the top of the barrel smoker with the fish attached. Light a fire of small sticks under the barrel and, once it is going, heap sawdust carefully around the sides, gradually working it over the flames. Adjust the draught by moving the bricks at the bottom of the barrel and when the fire is smouldering – producing more smoke than flame – cover the barrel with a damp sack and leave. Check the fire every hour or so, add more sawdust and adjust the draught if necessary (by moving the bricks at the bottom of the barrel and by removing the sack from time to time).

For small-scale hot-smoking – for example, of trout (or meaty items such as sausages) – a portable smoker is quite useful. The best-known is the Abu Smokebox, manufactured by Abu Svangsta in Sweden, but other types are now on the market. This is basically a small box which is lined with fine sawdust and heated by a methylated spirit burner. The fish is laid on a rack and the food is usually cooked and hot-smoked within about 20 minutes. This system produces much higher temperatures than those needed for conventional hot-smoking, so the fish is usually well cooked but has only a slightly smoky flavour. These portable smokers come with detailed instructions and are very easy to use. They are also handy for fishing trips and barbecues.

8 Cooling

Once the fish has been smoked, it needs to be left to cool. While cooling, it loses more weight and dries out. If smoked fish is packed or stored directly after curing, it will be moist and soft and is likely to turn mouldy.

9 Storing

Although fish smoking is a method of preservation, today's curing methods are quite mild and most items will keep in prime condition for only a few days. Cold-smoked fish tend to keep best; hot-smoked fish such as trout should be eaten within 3 days. The cool, even temperature of a larder is ideal for storing smoked fish – particularly if there is also a good circulation of air. Otherwise the fish can be wrapped in aluminium foil and stored in the refrigerator for about 7 days.

SMOKED SPRATS

This is a remunerative business when conducted on the best principles, employing children at trifling wages. I have found the following to be the best method. Provide a wooden trough eight feet long by a yard wide, and eighteen inches deep; fix strips of wood an inch square along the sides, lengthwise of the vat, and six inches above one another. On these will rest the spits which must be of iron wire, a yard long, and so as just to go within the vat. Pick out all the small fish and rubbish, but not too many at once, as they are apt to sweat if lying long together, and then would never be bright when smoked. Use a saturated solution of common salt, or, preferably, of rock salt, and if you intend to produce 'bloated sprats', two hours will be sufficient to let them remain in pickle; run off the brine, and put the fish on the spits, which may be a little pointed at one end. Hang them in a free current of air till next day, and smoke them with oak lops 2 parts, sawdust 2 parts, beech or birch chips 2 parts, until they are the colour of new sovereigns. These will not keep more than four or five days, and are generally esteemed. If you want *dried* sprats for commerce, let them remain in brine four hours, dry them well when on the spits, in a current of air, and when they begin to lose their plumpness, smoke them with similar fuel till the colour of Spanish mahogany. These when packed in boxes, like cigar boxes, will suit for exportation to the European continent, where many thousands of boxes are sent every winter.

(From *The Art & Mystery of Curing, Preserving & Potting*
by A Wholesale Curer of Comestibles, 1864.)

This was the wholesale method of smoking sprats in the nineteenth century. A century later the process is virtually unchanged, although most commercial curers use special kilns – and in Germany (where smoked sprats are called *Kielersprotten*) the fish are hot-smoked, fully cooked and then canned in oil.

Sprats are plentiful during the winter and spring. They are ideal for smoking and are the cheapest way of getting to know the process. Smoked sprats need only brown bread and butter, some wedges of lemon and a sprinkling of cayenne pepper. Good beer is the ideal thirst-quencher. If you want the sprats hot, they can be grilled or rolled in flour and deep-fried.

Sort through the fish, throwing out any that are damaged or past their best. Wash well in water and scrape off any scales, but keep the fish whole. Put into brine (see page 99) for 10–15 minutes, depending on their size, making sure that they are submerged.

Take the sprats out of the brine, and thread on to thin metal rods or thick wire – passed through the eye sockets or, if the fish are quite large, through the mouth and gills. Hang up to drip and dry in a cool airy place for about 1 hour. Then transfer to the smoker and cold-smoke over oak or beech for about 4 hours. They should not be too heavily cured otherwise they will become dry. Aim for a light golden colour and flesh that is firm and very slightly cooked (this is almost inevitable with small fish, even when the smoke temperature is quite low).

Remove from the smoker when sufficiently cured, allow to cool and store in a cool place. Eat within 5–7 days.

KIPPERS

In 1843, or thereabouts, John Woodger – a fish curer from Seahouses in Northumberland – devised a special method for cold-smoking herrings. He split them down the backbone, brined them and pinned them up to smoke over oak fires. These were the first kippers, destined to become the most popular and best-known of all smoked fish. Curers set up in business close to ports that serviced the seasonal herring fleets: in Northumberland itself, on the Isle of Man, along the west coast of Scotland – especially near Loch Fyne – and around Great Yarmouth and Lowestoft in East Anglia.

Experts agree that the best kippers are made from herrings with a high fat content: the big Norwegian fish are ideal for the job. Buy direct from the fishermen if you live on the coast, or use a reliable fishmonger.

Kippers can be grilled, poached (by steeping them in a jug of boiling water) or baked in aluminium foil. Butter and plenty of black pepper are essential, and thick slices of brown bread plus a mug of tea are ideal accompaniments. Another delicious way of eating kippers is to spread them with mustard. They can also be marinated in vinegar or lemon juice and olive oil and served in salads.

Wash and scrape any loose scales off the herrings and split the fish by making a cut along the right-hand side of the backbone from the back of the head to the tail. Turn the fish round, then make another cut, so that the head is split in the same way. Fold open the fish and remove and discard the guts and any roe. Wash well.

Steep the fish in a solution of brine (see page 99) for 15–30 minutes depending on their size and the thickness of the flesh. Then hang them up to dry in a cool airy place for 1 hour. You can thread some strong wire through the eye sockets, but a more reliable method is to pin the flesh on 'tenterhooks' pierced through the thick shoulder flesh. (Improvise with wooden poles or rods stuck with nails at regular intervals.) This method holds the fish open so that it is well exposed to smoke; there is also less chance of the flesh tearing at the head and falling into the fire.

Once the fish is suitably dried, transfer to your smoker and cold-smoke, preferably over oak chippings and sawdust, for about 6 hours, tending the fire and moving the fish around so that they are evenly cured. Remove from the smoke and hang up in a cool place until the kippers are cold. Store in a cool place and eat within 7 days.

SMOKED SALMON

It's possible that some sort of primitive salmon-smoking industry existed in Ireland in neolithic times. Remains have been found on the banks of the River Bann which suggest that groups of people visited the area on seasonal fishing trips, trapped the salmon in a weir and smoked them on the spot. The process of 'kippering' or smoking whole salmon after they had spawned became popular in the Middle Ages and lasted until early Victorian times.

But tastes were changing, and so was the increasingly refined flavour of mild-smoked salmon. It became a luxury, highly prized by the rich, who often demanded that the fish was cured over expensive cedarwood or even mahogany. Today's smoked salmon has continued this trend, although as the price of farmed fish continues to fall, it is an increasingly affordable treat.

Home-smoking salmon is not a task for beginners. If you have the experience and confidence, however, it is worth trying. Smoked salmon is at its best carved thinly and served with lemon wedges and brown bread and butter. But scraps or off-cuts can be turned into pâtés and mousses, or used to flavour omelettes, scrambled eggs, quiches and salads.

Starting with a whole fish, first scrape off any scales, remove the head and cut the body into two 'sides', working your knife along the backbone on each side of the fins. Leave the lug (collarbone) at the head end of each side and remove as many small bones as possible with a pair of tweezers. Clean the sides, removing any blood or dark skin from the belly area. Tie a piece of heavy thread or string in a loop through the shoulder flesh and under the lug bone (to enable the side to be hung up later). If you have part of a salmon, a tail end or other cut, prepare the fish in a similar fashion so that you have fillet pieces ready for curing.

Put a 1 inch (2.5 cm) layer of sea salt on to a shallow dish or tray that will contain the fish and lay the salmon – skin side down – on this. If you are curing two sides together, lay them adjacent to each other. Cover the salmon with a layer of salt. At the head end, where the flesh is thickest, you will need a layer about 1 inch (2.5 cm) thick, tapering off towards the tail, where ½ inch (1 cm) should be sufficient. (If you want to spice or flavour the salt, mix it with, say, 2 oz (50 g) brown sugar, 1 tablespoon (1 × 15 ml spoon) dark rum, or 1 teaspoon (1 × 5 ml spoon) crushed juniper berries – the choice is yours.) The salting time depends mainly on the weight per side: for instance, 1½–2 lb (750 g–1 kg) will need 6–8 hours, while 6 lb (2.75 kg) will need 18 hours. Cover the dish and leave in a cool airy place until the salmon is sufficiently salted, making sure that the flesh is always covered with the salt mixture.

Remove the fish from the tray and wash it free of excess salt. Then hang it up by the loop of thread for 1 hour in a dry airy place.

The fish is now ready to smoke. Transfer it to the smoking barrel and suspend it by its loop or lay it flat on a wire rack, depending on its size. It should be cold-smoked, preferably over oak, beech or birch, for about 12 hours. Very large sides may need longer, but always aim for a light cure. Don't oversmoke or the fish will dry out and lose its plumpness. Remove from the smoke when ready and hang up in a dry place to cool. Then store in a cool place until needed. Smoked salmon will keep well for 5–7 days, especially if wrapped in aluminium foil once you have started carving it.

SMOKED TROUT

Smoked trout first appeared on the market about 20 years ago, as trout farms started to look for an extra outlet for their fish. However, if you want to smoke your own, always try to use wild rather than farmed fish – which can be very bland and dry.

The classic accompaniment for smoked trout is horseradish sauce or a mayonnaise flavoured with horseradish and lemon juice. It can also be turned into a pâté or mousse.

Wash the fish well to remove the slimy coating that covers the skin. Keep the fish whole, but split open the belly and take out the guts, making sure you get rid of any blood and black skin near the backbone. Rinse well.

Put the fish into brine (see page 99) for about 1 hour, making sure that they are submerged during this time. Take them out and thread them on to thick wire or thin metal rods pierced through the eye sockets. Keep the belly flaps apart by fitting a matchstick across each one – this helps the smoke to penetrate more quickly. Put the fish to smoke straight away, while they are still wet. (This is important because trout flesh has very little fat and soon hardens if it is allowed to dry out.)

Hot-smoke the fish over ash or birch for about 3 hours by raising the temperature to around 180°F (82°C). Controlling the fire and the temperature is the main problem. If the fire flares up too quickly, the fish will char and burn before it is properly cured. If the temperature is too low, the fish will not be sufficiently cooked, though you can remedy this by finishing it off in a very low oven.

Allow the fish to cool, then store in a cool dry place and eat within 4 days.

CHAPTER NINE

KETCHUPS, CONDIMENTS AND DRESSINGS

KETCHUPS AND SAUCES

The word 'ketchup' comes from the Chinese '*koe-chiap*', a pickled fish sauce that was later introduced into South-east Asia and India by travellers and immigrants. But it was not until the last years of the seventeenth century that any of these products found their way to England. Traders from the East India Company discovered them and brought back samples – including the first batches of soy sauce.

The flavours and pungency of these sauces inspired English cooks and housekeepers, and before long they were devising their own range of bottled condiments. At first these were often no more than the liquor left from jars of pickles. So walnut pickle became walnut 'catchup', and the liquid from pickled mushrooms was re-named mushroom 'catchup'. Although the original products from the Orient were fish sauces, these English counterparts had the same dark potency. Soon special recipes started to emerge, often including salted anchovies as one of their ingredients, giving a more authentic flavour to these 'store sauces' (a title used to distinguish them from classic sauces made to accompany specific dishes).

By the nineteenth century there were scores of recipes for these sauces, but most were simply permutations of anchovies, soy, horseradish, vinegar and spices, sold under different names: Pontac's sauce, Quin's sauce and – of course – Worcestershire sauce. Another favourite was Harvey's sauce. The story of its 'invention' suggests more than a hint of sharp practice.

> Captain Charles Combers . . . stopped, as was his wont, to dine at The George at Bedford, then kept by a man named Harvey, where he ordered a steak, and when it was served Combers requested Harvey to let his servant bring from his buggy a quart bottle which contained an admirable sauce. Combers poured some of it on to his plate and having mixed it with the gravy of the steak he asked Harvey to taste it, and the host pronounced it to be a most excellent dish.
>
> 'Well, Mr Harvey,' said Combers, 'I shall leave the bottle with you to use till my return, only be careful to reserve enough for me.'
>
> On the next day Harvey had to provide a wedding dinner, and introduced the sauce which afforded such general satisfaction, that several small parties were made up and the contents of the bottle were soon exhausted. In due course Captain Combers returned, and having been told no more remained, said, 'Never mind, I can make some more from my mother's recipe, and by the by, I'll give you a copy of it.' He did so. Harvey made it in large quantities, sent it to different shops in London, advertised it as Harvey's Sauce and by its extensive sale realised a large income – he subsequently sold the recipe for an annuity of £400 or £500 a year.
>
> (From *The Quorn Hunt and its Masters* by W. C. A. Blew
> – quoted in *Good Things in England* by Florence White,
> Jonathan Cape, 1932.)

These days, the word 'ketchup' usually describes a thick pulpy sauce not unlike a puréed chutney. Tomato ketchup is ubiquitous – along with anonymous 'brown sauce'. Some commercial versions of these products are acceptable, others are truly awful; manufacturers have made an effort to reduce additives in their products, but there's no substitute for the home-made article with its flavour and pungent spiciness.

GUIDELINES FOR MAKING KETCHUPS

1 Basic rules

(a) Use stainless-steel pans and utensils and wooden spoons. Avoid copper, brass or aluminium.

(b) Even though the ingredients will be chopped and cooked to a pulp, they must be of good quality.

(c) Ketchups need longer cooking than chutneys, so that the fruit and vegetables are reduced to a pulp and will pour easily. Remember that ketchups tend to thicken as they cool.

(d) Make ketchups in small batches, so that they can be used up quickly once opened.

2 Sterilising the bottles

It is advisable to sterilise most ketchups and sauces after bottling, since there is always the possible risk of fermentation – particularly when tomatoes and mushrooms are involved.

Choose bottles that will withstand the heat necessary to sterilise the ketchup. Old sauce bottles with a plastic screw cap are ideal. If other bottles are used, they can be fitted with corks, but these need to be tied down. Wash the bottles, caps or corks, then boil in water for 30 minutes: this is important, otherwise corks may go mouldy during storage. Remove the bottles from the water – the long handle of a clean wooden spoon can be used to lift them out. Drain excess water out of the bottles and put them on to a wooden surface (not cold marble or tiles).

3 Bottling the ketchup

Pour the hot ketchup into the bottles, using a funnel, and fill to within 1 inch (2.5 cm) of the top. Lightly seal or cork at once. Line a large pan of water with plenty of newspaper or a false bottom and put the bottles in upright. Some extra newspaper between them will help to keep them in place. The water level must come up to the neck of the bottles.

Bring the water to the boil and simmer at 190°F (88°C) for 20 minutes, or at 170°F (77°C) for 30 minutes. (If you are unable to check the temperature with a thermometer, let the water boil vigorously for at least 15 minutes.) You may need to top up the water level from time to time. Remove the hot bottles with an oven cloth, tighten the screw caps or secure the corks and leave to cool. If you want an extra seal, dip the necks of the cooled bottles in melted paraffin wax.

4   Storing

Ketchups and sauces should be stored in a cool dry place until needed. Once opened, some ketchups, such as tomato, need to be used up quite quickly; most 'store sauces' will keep almost indefinitely.

TOMATO KETCHUP

Home-made tomato ketchup has a taste totally unlike most commercial versions. Fresh ripe tomatoes make all the difference, and the ketchup gets its character from the different spices and seasonings.

Makes about 5–6 lb (2.25–2.75 kg)

6 lb (2.75 kg) ripe tomatoes, roughly chopped
1 onion, chopped
3 cloves garlic, chopped
1 teaspoon (1 × 5 ml spoon) paprika
1 teaspoon (1 × 5 ml spoon) cayenne pepper

juice 1 orange
1 teaspoon (1 × 5 ml spoon) sea salt
8 oz (225 g) white sugar
10 fl oz (300 ml) cider vinegar

Put the tomatoes, onion and garlic into a preserving pan and cook very slowly on a low heat, stirring well to prevent sticking, until the mixture is soft and pulpy. Add all the other ingredients and continue to cook until the mixture has a thick, even consistency. Then sieve or liquidise until you have a smooth lump-free ketchup. (Remember that the ketchup will thicken as it cools.)

Pour the hot ketchup into clean warmed bottles, seal and put them into a pan of hot water to sterilise (see page 109). After 30 minutes remove the bottles, tighten the caps securely and store in a cool dark place. The ketchup will keep for at least 3 months, but once opened it should be stored in the fridge and used up quickly.

MUSHROOM KETCHUP

On 4 October 1779 the naturalist and diarist Gilbert White noted in his journal: 'Mushrooms abound. Made catchup.' The best mushrooms for making ketchup are large, black, flat, field mushrooms, which yield plenty of highly flavoured juice. Collect them from the wild on a dry day: wet or damp mushrooms soon decay and the resulting ketchup can ferment or go off quickly.

Mushroom ketchup is a very useful flavouring for soups, stews and casseroles.

Makes about 2 pints (1.2 litres)

3 lb (1.5 kg) mushrooms
3 oz (75 g) sea salt
½ teaspoon (½ × 5 ml spoon)
  ground mace
½ teaspoon (½ × 5 ml spoon)
  ground ginger

1 teaspoon (1 × 5 ml spoon)
  freshly ground black pepper
1 pint (600 ml) red wine vinegar
2 tablespoons (2 × 15 ml spoons)
  port

Do not wash the mushrooms. Simply remove the base of the stalks and wipe the caps with a damp cloth. Break them into pieces, put into a bowl and sprinkle with sea salt. Leave in a cool place overnight.

Next day strain off excess liquid from the mushrooms, put them into an ovenproof dish and mash them up with a wooden spoon. Add the spices and vinegar. Cover the dish and cook in the oven at gas mark 3, 325°F (160°C), for 30 minutes.

Remove the mushrooms from the oven, then strain through a sieve, reserving the juice. Discard the mushrooms. Add the port to the juice, then pour into clean warmed bottles. Sterilise in a pan of hot water for 30 minutes in the usual way (see page 109). Remove from the water, seal the caps securely and store in a cool dark place. This ketchup should keep for several months without deteriorating.

QUIN'S FISH SAUCE

The original version of this fish sauce featured in the first edition of *The Art of Cookery Made Plain & Easy* by Hannah Glasse in 1747. It contained 24 anchovies, 1 quart (1.2 litres) white wine, 1 pint (600 ml) red wine, 10 shallots and a handful of scraped horseradish as well as lemon and spices. The boast was that it would keep for a whole year. Later the recipe was toned down, and this is an adapted version for today's kitchens.

Thickened with a little butter and flour, it can be used as a potent accompaniment to boiled fowl and veal.

Makes about 10 fl oz (300 ml)

2 shallots, finely chopped
3 tinned anchovy fillets, finely chopped
5 fl oz (150 ml) mushroom ketchup (see page 111)
2½ fl oz (65 ml) walnut pickle

2½ fl oz (65 ml) port
1 tablespoon (1 × 15 ml spoon) soy sauce
½ teaspoon (½ × 5 ml spoon) cayenne pepper

Mix together the chopped shallots and anchovy fillets. Put into a pan and add the other ingredients. Simmer for about 15 minutes.

Remove from the heat and allow to cool. Transfer to clean warmed bottles, seal and store in a cool dark place for at least 1 month, shaking from time to time.

ELDERBERRY KETCHUP

The story goes that there was once a hostelry in London's Lombard Street, where Samuel Pepys first drank Château Haut Brion. It was on the site of this tavern that Monsieur Pontac – owner of the *château* – set up his famous eating house. One of his specialities was Pontac's sauce, made appropriately from claret and elderberries. In a modified form this became one of the famous of all 'store sauces'.

The nineteenth-century cookery writer Eliza Acton recommended using elderberry ketchup with fish. Its sharp fruity taste also acts as a good foil to liver and kidneys.

Makes about 1 pint (600 ml)

2 pints (1.2 litres) ripe elderberries (prepared quantity)
10 fl oz (300 ml) white wine vinegar or cider vinegar
4 shallots, finely minced

1 teaspoon (1 × 5 ml spoon) sea salt
6 cloves
2 teaspoons (2 × 5 ml spoons) black peppercorns
2 slices fresh root ginger

Collect the elderberries when they are fully ripe. Strip the berries off the stalks, discarding any rotten ones along with bits of leaf and rubbish. Put into a non-metallic ovenproof dish with the vinegar. Cover and cook at the bottom of the oven at gas mark 2, 300°F (150°C), for about 30 minutes, then remove and leave to steep overnight.

Next day, strain the juice into a preserving pan, add the minced shallots, salt and spices. Boil for 10 minutes, then pour through a sieve. Transfer to thoroughly cleaned bottles, seal well and store in a cool dark place. (There is no need to sterilise this ketchup.)

Pontac's sauce had a legendary reputation for longevity: it was meant to be stored for 7 years before being opened. Without doubt it keeps extremely well.

WORCESTERSHIRE SAUCE

In 1835 Lord Sandys, returning to England from India (where he had been Governor of Bengal), walked into a chemist's in Worcester with a saucy recipe he had acquired in the East. The shop was owned by Messrs Lea and Perrins and they duly obliged, blending vinegar, salt, garlic and spices and following the instructions to the letter.

They were curious men and kept a few gallons of the sauce for themselves. It tasted awful, so they put it into their cellar and forgot about it. Some two years later they tasted it again and found it transformed. Worcestershire sauce was born.

The recipe is still a secret, known only to a few privileged members of the Lea & Perrins factory in Worcester. Consequently, imitations abound. This version produces something close to the original.

Makes about 1¼ pints (750 ml)

2 oz (50 g) shallots, roughly chopped
4 cloves garlic, roughly chopped
1 pint (600 ml) malt vinegar
2 teaspoons (2 × 5 ml spoons) grated horseradish (preferably fresh)
2 teaspoons (2 × 5 ml spoons) cayenne pepper
6 cloves

4 slices fresh root ginger
4 cardamom seeds
2 teaspoons (2 × 5 ml spoons) black peppercorns
1 teaspoon (1 × 5 ml spoon) anchovy essence
4 fl oz (100 ml) soy sauce
2 teaspoons (2 × 5 ml spoons) dark Muscovado sugar

Boil the shallots and garlic in the vinegar in a stainless-steel pan for 15 minutes. Add all the other ingredients, cover the pan and simmer for a further 30 minutes. Transfer to a clean warmed bottle with a narrow neck, seal and keep in a cool dark place for at least 1 month, shaking from time to time. Test the sauce. If it is not fully flavoured, leave for another month. Then re-bottle and use as required.

FLAVOURED OILS

Good-quality oils – olive, walnut, hazelnut, sesame and so on – should be part of every larder. It is also very easy and interesting to devise different-flavoured oils for use in salad dressings, stir-frying and to give a final glaze to sautéed dishes. Use a rather bland oil – such as soya or sunflower – as the base, so that it does not compete with the other flavourings.

GARLIC AND GINGER OIL

Makes about 1 pint (600 ml)

6 cloves garlic, chopped
2 oz (50 g) fresh root ginger,
   sliced

1 pint (600 ml) soya or sunflower
   oil

Put the garlic and ginger into a screw-top jar or a narrow-necked bottle (whichever is more convenient). Add the oil. Shake well and leave in a cool dark place for at least 14 days, shaking from time to time.

If you want a mild flavour, strain off the oil and re-bottle. Otherwise leave the whole lot to steep and it will increase in strength as time passes.

CHILLI OIL

One of the essential flavourings for Chinese and South-east Asian cooking. It has all manner of uses: for example, drizzle it over cold sesame chicken and cucumber or add it as a final potent flourish to Indonesian laksa (coconut soup with noodles).

Makes about 1 pint (600 ml)

2 teaspoons (2 × 5 ml spoons)
   dried red chillies
4 cloves garlic

6 dried shrimps (optional)
1 pint (600 ml) soya or sunflower
   oil

Crush the chillies roughly to liberate the heat from the seeds. Chop the garlic and crush the dried shrimps. Put into a screw-top jar or a narrow-necked bottle and fill up with oil.

Shake well, then leave well for about 4 weeks to steep in a cool dark place. The oil will gradually darken and become reddish in colour as it matures. Leave it as long as you dare: it needs to be very strong.

HERB OIL

John Tovey, of Miller Howe Hotel in Windermere, is one of the most inventive and flamboyant chefs in the business and his cooking is dominated by unusual vivid flavours. Not surprisingly he takes full advantage of the possibilities of different oils:

> Use as much as you like of any chopped herb, or a mixture. Basil is one of my favourites, and whenever my basil plants are about to give up the ghost each year, I religiously strip off every single leaf and press them into my jars and cover them with oil. After a few weeks, the oil gives a bouncing basil flavour to remind me of the erstwhile summer. (And if you liquidise some toasted pine kernels with a clove of garlic and some of this oil, it makes a delightful spread for cold white meats.)

> (From *The Miller Howe Cookbook* by John Tovey,
> Century Hutchinson, 1987.)

FLAVOURED VINEGARS

Like oils, flavoured vinegars are part and parcel of a good larder. There are several distinct types. Herb vinegars are made quite simply by steeping different herbs in vinegar until it is well flavoured. The resulting liquor can be used for pickles, dressings and sauces. Fruit vinegars are renowned as cordials – either hot for the relief of sore throats, or ice-cold as reviving summer drinks. There are lots of possibilities and you can experiment with different combinations of herbs, fruit and vinegars to produce a range of flavours for the kitchen. Flavoured vinegars look beautiful too.

ROSEMARY VINEGAR

An unusual pink vinegar that can be decorated with a firm sprig of fresh rosemary.

Makes about 1 pint (600 ml)

2 oz (50 g) fresh rosemary sprigs
5 fl oz (150 ml) red wine vinegar
15 fl oz (450 ml) white wine
    vinegar

1 sprig fresh rosemary to decorate

Pick the rosemary just before it flowers, when the flavour and fragrance are at their peak. Strip off the leaves and pack into a screw-top jar or bottle. Cover with the cold vinegar mixture and leave to steep for about 2 weeks. Then strain off into a new bottle (preferably long and narrow) and slip in a sprig of fresh rosemary for decoration. Cover and store in a cool dark place until required.

APRICOT VINEGAR

A deliciously scented, golden-coloured vinegar which can be decorated with strips of lemon and orange peel. Unlike most fruit vinegars, it is made without sugar.

Makes about 1 pint (600 ml)

8 oz (225 g) dried apricots
1 pint (600 ml) white wine
    vinegar

1 strip lemon rind
1 strip orange rind

Chop the apricots and put them into a bowl. Cover with the vinegar and leave to steep for 3 days, mashing with a wooden spoon from time to time. Strain carefully through a jelly bag (see page 129), allowing the liquid to drip through at its own pace.

Transfer the vinegar to a clean bottle and curl in a strip each of lemon and orange rind for decoration as well as flavour. Store in a cool dark place until required.

BLACKBERRY VINEGAR

A rich soothing vinegar, given added character with honey. It is a good way of using up slightly overripe fruit.

Makes about 1½ pints (900 ml)

1 pint (600 ml) ripe blackberries
1 pint (600 ml) white wine
   vinegar

1 lb (450 g) white sugar
8 oz (225 g) thin honey

Sort through the blackberries, discarding any that are blemished or rotten. Wash well, drain, then put into a bowl with the vinegar. Cover and steep for about 1 week, stirring from time to time.

Strain the liquid through a jelly bag (see page 129) and put into a stainless-steel pan. Add the sugar and honey, stir well and bring to the boil. Once the mixture has reached boiling point, remove from the heat and allow to cool. Pour into clean bottles and store in a cool dark place.

DRESSINGS

The first salad dressings were seasoned sauces used to accompany assortments of raw and cooked vegetables, herbs and leaves. Needless to say, the Romans developed the idea and had different dressings for different vegetables: endives with 'liquamen' (the essential fish sauce), a little oil, wine and chopped onion; radishes with a pepper dressing; lettuces with a powerful concoction of cumin, ginger, rue, pepper, honey and vinegar.

By the Middle Ages there were precise recipes for salads, like this one dating from 1393:

Salad. Take parsley, sage, garlic, chibols [Welsh onions], onions, leeks, borage, mints, porray [a herb purée], fennel, and garden cresses, rue, rosemary, purslain; lave and wash them clean; pick them, pluck them small with thine hand, and mingle them well with raw oil. Lay on vinegar and salt and serve it forth.

Sometimes the dressing might be given more body by the addition of bread steeped in vinegar, but the principle of oil, vinegar and salt – sometimes with other herbs or spices – has remained virtually unchanged for hundreds of years. It was also quite common to include sugar in dressing recipes, although John Evelyn was pleased to see the end of this practice: 'Now sugar is almost wholly banished from all, except the more effeminate palates, as too much palling, and taking from the grateful acid now in use.' In his classic treatise on salads, *Acetaria* (1699), he favoured an artful combination of three parts olive oil, one of vinegar (or lemon or orange juice), some dry mustard and mashed hard-boiled egg yolks.

From here it was a short gastronomic step to the salad sauce or salad cream that has swamped platefuls of lettuce and tomatoes in England for more than a century. Dr William Kitchiner can take much of the credit for devising the precursor of this dressing. His 1817 recipe includes hard-boiled egg yolks, cream, olive oil, salt, mustard and vinegar. Oddly, he recommends water as an alternative to cream, melted butter to olive oil and sugar to salt. If properly made, this was a creditable condiment, but once the food technologists got hold of the idea it soon became – in Elizabeth David's words – 'one of the major culinary disasters of this country'.

GREEN HERB DRESSING

In the fifteenth century this would have been called 'verde sawse' (green sauce). It is a marvellous dressing provided that you use freshly picked herbs at their peak.

Makes about 4 fl oz (120 ml)

2 tablespoons (2 × 15 ml spoons) chopped fresh parsley

1 tablespoon (1 × 15 ml spoon) chopped fresh chives

1 teaspoon (1 × 5 ml spoon) chopped fresh mint

1 teaspoon (1 × 5 ml spoon) chopped fresh chervil

1 clove garlic, crushed

2 fl oz (50 ml) olive oil

2 tablespoons (2 × 15 ml spoons) cider vinegar or white wine vinegar

1 tablespoon (1 × 15 ml spoon) lemon juice

sea salt and freshly ground black pepper to taste

Sort through the herbs, wash and drain them well. Chop finely and mix in a bowl with the crushed garlic. Carefully blend in the oil, vinegar and lemon juice. Season to taste with salt and pepper. Use straight away, or transfer to a bottle, seal and store until required.

OXFORD BRAWN SAUCE

'Brawne and mustarde' was one of the great festive dishes of the Middle Ages. Often the mustard was actually a sauce or dressing compounded with oil and vinegar. This is an excellent addition to the larder, rather like dark honey in appearance, and equally good with cold spiced beef as well as brawn.

Makes about 8 fl oz (250 ml)

2 oz (50 g) soft brown sugar
2 teaspoons (2 × 5 ml spoons) prepared English mustard
½ teaspoon (½ × 5 ml spoon) sea salt
pinch of freshly ground black pepper
4 fl oz (120 ml) olive oil
2 fl oz (60 ml) cider vinegar

Blend together the sugar, mustard and seasoning. Add the oil and mix well. Transfer to a clean bottle and pour in the vinegar. Seal and shake well so that the ingredients mingle together thoroughly. Store in a cool dark place until required.

CHAPTER TEN

PRESERVES

JAMS

The forerunners of today's jams were the so-called 'marmalades' that started to appear in the Middle Ages. At first these were made from spicy mixtures of fruit and honey, but by the sixteenth century sugar had started to find its way into British kitchens. Plums, damsons, pears, apples and strawberries, as well as rarer fruit such as medlars and service berries, were all turned into preserves. The fruit was cooked until soft, sieved to a pulp, then mixed with sugar and boiled until it thickened. The result was not a spread, but a solid sweetmeat eaten in lumps after meals.

By the beginning of the eighteenth century it was the practice simply to bruise and boil soft fruit in sugar syrup without any straining or sieving. These preserves were called 'jams' – the word first appeared in cookery books around 1718. They quickly found favour in middle-class and upper-class households with large gardens and orchards, enough money to buy sugar in bulk, plus cooks and other servants to do the chopping, boiling and potting.

In the last years of the nineteenth century jam-making moved from the kitchen to the factory. Cheap manufactured jams appeared in towns and cities largely as a result of the agricultural depression that forced farmers to find new markets for unwanted fruit. They were dubious concoctions prepared from fruit and vegetable pulp with added sugar, colour and flavouring. Their manufacture was a primitive and dangerous business, judging by Charles Booth's description in his survey *Life and Labour of the People of London* (published 1889–1903):

> Jam-making is ordinarily the work of men as regards mixing and boiling, and the work of women for filling, covering and labelling the pots; in some factories women are employed to attend to the boiling, the work being made possible for them by the use of steam . . . women and girls are often badly burnt, either from the bursting of a jar whilst it is being filled with the boiling liquid, or owing to a slip when conveying heavy loads of scalding jam from the furnace to the cooling-room.

By 1900 jam sales had rocketed. Jam had become a staple food for poor families because it was a cheap, colourful addition to a dreary larder; it provided an alternative to fresh fruit, and – like highly spiced sauces and relishes – masked the poor quality of most daily bread. Schools, factories and prisons all provided jam for their inmates and workers: it was the perfect intitutional food for authorities that were unwilling to spend more than a minute sum on feeding the poor.

Jam today is very different. Working conditions in jam factories have improved, although there's no escaping the heat, noise and bubbling activity of the huge vats. Quality has improved too, yet commercial jam-makers still use preservatives, anti-oxidants, colourants and artificial flavourings in many of their products. There is also a question mark over the freshness and condition of the fruit used by some producers. All of this can be avoided, of course, if you make your own.

GUIDELINES FOR MAKING JAM

1 Principles and practice

To make good jam you need to have pectin, acid and sugar present in the correct proportions.

Pectin occurs in varying amounts in the cell walls of fruit. It is important to extract as much pectin as possible from the fruit when it is boiled, as this is essential for setting. If all fruit had the same pectin content, jam-making would be easy. But the amount varies, not only from one type of fruit to another, but also from variety to variety; it also depends on ripeness. High-pectin fruit includes apples, gooseberries, blackcurrants, redcurrants and damsons. Medium-pectin fruit includes plums, greengages, raspberries, apricots and loganberries. Low-pectin fruit includes strawberries, cherries, blackberries, pears, rhubarb, haws and rowan berries; and vegetables such as marrow and carrots, that are also sometimes made into jam, are low in pectin too.

Fruit that is high in pectin will make the best jam. It is usually necessary to add a little extra acid for fruit with medium setting, while that which is low or lacking in pectin needs an additional source before it will set. The easiest way to provide this is to add a pectin-rich fruit such as apples – either as the whole fruit or in the form of juice.

Acid is necessary for the proper extraction of pectin and aids setting. It also improves the colour and flavour of jam and helps to prevent sugar crystallising out once the jam has been made. Acid is present in most fruits in varying amounts, but if extra is needed, a convenient source is lemon or lime juice; other fruit such as redcurrants and gooseberries are also useful.

Sugar is used as a preservative and a sweetener. It is also necessary for a good set. Jams can be made using only the natural sugar in the fruit, but these tend to be sloppy and don't keep well for long periods. It is important to include the correct amount of sugar: too much *or* too little will give a poor result. Use white 'preserving sugar' (which dissolves quickly) or brown sugar, depending on the recipe.

2   Equipment

Make jam in a stainless-steel saucepan or a large two-handled preserving pan. Avoid aluminium, copper or iron. It is a mistake to try to make too much jam in one session, so aim to have your pan no more than two thirds full once the sugar has been added.

You will need a supply of jars. These should be cleaned in boiling water with washing-up liquid, put upside down on a clean cloth to drain, then left to dry and warm at the bottom of a cool oven pre-heated to gas mark 1 or 2, 275–300°F (140–150°C), until needed. Don't dry the insides of the jars with a cloth as this may do more harm than good by spreading bacteria. The jars must be warm, not hot.

The simplest way to cover the jars is to use wax discs and circles of clear plastic. These can be purchased from most hardware stores, kitchen shops and large stationers. Alternatively you can buy direct from Lakeland Plastics, Alexandra Buildings, Station Precinct, Windermere, Cumbria LA23

1BQ, which supplies the full range of preserving accessories. (Plastic twist-on tops are also suitable in most cases.) In addition you will need wooden spoons (preferably flat-bottomed) and a stainless-steel perforated spoon for skimming. A jam thermometer is useful for testing setting points, but it isn't essential.

3   The basic method

(a) Start with good-quality fresh fruit. Discard any that are damaged or blemished. Harvest fruit from the garden or the wild on a dry day: damp or wet fruit will decay quickly and this affects the jam. The fruit should be just ripe, when pectin is at its peak.

(b) Simmer the fruit gently to soften it and to break down the cell walls. It may be necessary to add a little water to prevent burning if the fruit needs a good deal of cooking. Soft fruit, such as raspberries, do not require any water. The idea is to extract as much pectin as possible without overcooking the fruit and losing its flavour.

(c) Warm the sugar in a very low oven before adding it to the fruit, as this helps it to dissolve more quickly. Remove the pan from the heat when adding the sugar so that it does not caramelise in a lump at the bottom of the pan. Stir well with a wooden spoon until dissolved, then return to the heat.

(d) Boil the jam rapidly until setting point is reached. There are several ways of gauging this. First you need to watch for 'a rolling boil' – that is, a bubbling activity in the jam that cannot be stirred out. This tells you that the jam is near to setting point. Then do a simple test. Remove the pan from the heat, take out a very small quantity of jam with a wooden spoon and put a drop on to a cold plate. As it cools the jam should begin to solidify and the surface should crinkle when pushed with a finger. If this happens, the jam is ready. If not, return to the heat for a few minutes, then try again.

Alternatively you can use a jam thermometer. Put this into hot water before testing. Stir the jam well and take a reading, making sure that the bulb of the thermometer is not touching the bottom of the pan. If the jam is boiled to 220°F (104.5°C) it will set; occasionally 221°F (105°C) or even 222°F (105.5°C) may give a better result.

If disaster strikes and the jam begins to burn, you will need to take the pan off the heat, clean it and start again. The situation will get worse if you don't act. Brown patches can be removed from the bottom of a stainless-steel pan by adding a couple of tablespoons (2 × 15 ml spoons) of washing soda crystals with about 10 fl oz (300 ml) water; bring the water to the boil and the burns will lift off.

(e) Remove any scum from the surface of the jam with a perforated spoon. Let the jam cool for a few minutes, then stir to disperse the fruit before pouring into jars. This prevents the fruit from rising to the surface as the jam sets.

(f) Cover the jam. Lay a waxed circle carefully on the surface of the jam, smoothing out any air bubbles. Then put a transparent cover over the jar and secure around the 'neck' with a rubber band. It is a good idea to moisten the *top* of the cover before using as this helps it to stretch.

(g) Label the jam with its name and the date. Store in a cool, dry, dark place until needed.

Rhubarb and Ginger Jam

The pulpy, slightly fibrous consistency of cooked rhubarb makes for an unusual jam, particularly when it is spiced up with ginger. As a variation try adding 4 oz (100 g) mixed peel to the jam: this gives it a sweetish, citrus tang.

Makes about 4 lb (1.75 kg)

2 lb (1 kg) rhubarb
2 lb (1 kg) white sugar
juice 2 lemons

½ oz (15 g) fresh root ginger, bruised

Clean and trim the rhubarb and cut into small pieces. Put into a stainless-steel bowl with the sugar, layer by layer, then add the lemon juice and leave to stand overnight.

Next day transfer the rhubarb and the syrupy juice that has formed into a preserving pan. Add the root ginger, tied in a piece of muslin. Bring to the boil and continue to cook for about 20 minutes, or until the jam has a good consistency and reaches setting point when tested. Remove the muslin, then pot the hot jam into clean, warmed jars. Cover and seal.

RASPBERRY JAM

If you have a crop of perfect, fresh-picked fruit, the best jam to make is this *uncooked* one.

Makes about 4 lb (1.75 kg)

2 lb (1 kg) white sugar   2 lb (1 kg) raspberries

Pre-heat the oven to gas mark ½, 250°F (120°C).

Put the sugar into an ovenproof dish and place at the bottom of the oven for about 10 minutes to warm. Check regularly to make sure that the sugar is not becoming too hot, otherwise it may start to caramelise.

Remove the bowl from the oven and add the raspberries. Mash well and mix in the fruit until the sugar has dissolved and the jam has an even, pulpy consistency. Pot and cover in the usual way. This jam should be stored in a cool place and used within 1 month.

MORELLO CHERRY AND WALNUT JAM

Dark Morello cherries are at their peak for a couple of weeks in the summer. Although they are sublime eaten fresh, they can also be turned into a preserve. This recipe is more like a conserve as the fruit is kept whole and other ingredients are added as well as sugar. Try it as a savoury relish with guinea fowl, goose or duck.

Makes about 4 lb (1.75 kg)

2 lb (1 kg) Morello cherries   1½ lb (750 g) white sugar
4 oz (100 g) raisins   2 oz (50 g) walnuts, chopped
juice 1 lemon

Remove all bits of stalk and leaf from the cherries and discard, along with any blemished fruit. Wash the cherries well, split open, remove the stones and tie these in a muslin bag.

Put the cherries, raisins and muslin bag of stones into a preserving pan with a very small amount of water. Simmer for about 10 minutes or until the fruit is soft. Remove the muslin bag and add the lemon juice and sugar. Stir well until the sugar has dissolved, then bring to the boil and cook until setting point is reached.

Stir in the chopped walnuts at the last moment, remove from the heat and allow the jam to cool a little. Pot into clean, warmed jars and seal in the usual way.

GOOSEBERRY AND ORANGE JAM

An unusual but delicious jam, the citrus tang of the oranges perfectly off-setting the mildness of the gooseberries. Always use firm, green, slightly underripe gooseberries.

Makes about 5 lb (2.25 kg)

3 lb (1.5 kg) green gooseberries
10 fl oz (300 ml) water

2 lb (1 kg) white sugar
juice 2 oranges

Top and tail the gooseberries – a pair of scissors is the best tool for the job. Wash them well and put into a pan with the water. Simmer until soft but not overcooked. Remove from the heat and stir in the warmed sugar and the orange juice.

Return to the heat, bring to the boil and cook vigorously until setting point is reached. Pot into clean, warmed jars and cover in the usual way.

APRICOT AND ALMOND JAM

Clare Benson runs an enterprising cottage industry from her farm at Rendcomb in Gloucestershire. She produces a wide range of jams, chutneys and marmalades under the Clare's Kitchen label as well as hummus, nut spreads and mustards. Her philosophy is simple and forward-looking: she obtains organically grown fruit and vegetables whenever possible and uses no preservatives or other artificial additives in her recipes.

This jam, one of Clare's, is unusual because it includes no added sugar: the apple juice provides its own sweetness. Clare uses sulphur-free apricots in keeping with her commitment to additive-free ingredients.

Makes about 2 lb (1 kg)

1 lb (450 g) dried apricots   1 oz (25 g) flaked almonds
1¾ pints (1 litre) concentrated
    apple juice

Chop the apricots and soak them in a bowl of cold water for at least 2 hours. Drain well. Put into a preserving pan over a low heat and stir until mushy. Mash well with a wooden spoon. Add a little water if the mixture looks as if it might burn.

Remove from the heat and pour in the apple juice. Stir well, return to the heat and boil until setting point is reached. Allow to cool a little, then stir in the flaked almonds. Cover and seal in the usual way.

CHESTNUT PRESERVE

Versatility is one of the virtues of the sweet chestnut (*Castanea sativa*). The nuts can be eaten straight from the shell, roasted, turned into *marrons glacées*, puréed or made into a preserve.

This preserve is best served as a savoury relish with cold turkey or game.

Makes about 3 lb (1.5 kg)

2 lb (1 kg) sweet chestnuts   2 teaspoons (2 × 5 ml spoons)
1½ lb (750 g) white sugar   vanilla essence
10 fl oz (300 ml) water

Slit the skins of the chestnuts and boil them in a little water for about 30 minutes or until they are tender. Peel them, then roughly grind in a food processor or press through a sieve. You can have a smooth or coarse-textured preserve depending on your taste.

Dissolve the sugar in 10 fl oz (300 ml) water, add the vanilla essence and boil until the mixture is thick and syrupy. Add the ground or sieved chestnuts and continue to boil for 10–15 minutes or until the preserve is thick and firm. Transfer the hot preserve to clean, warmed jars, and cover in the usual way. Store in a completely dry, cool place and eat within 2 weeks.

JELLIES

Fruit jellies started to become popular in the sixteenth century, but they were nothing like today's preserves. Strawberries, raspberries and mulberries were crushed in a mortar with sugar, then boiled up with a mixture of water, rosewater and isinglass; after sieving, the solid jelly was put into boxes and kept for a year. No wonder the Elizabethans, with their fondness for colourful conceits, found these sweetmeats irresistible.

Later the more familiar method of boiling the fruit, straining the juice and mixing it with sugar, started to find favour, especially in the case of fruits such as gooseberries and barberries that are rich in pectin. Although these jellies were sometimes used as sweet preserves, the real English tradition was to serve them as accompaniments to meat, poultry and game. This idea has survived in such classic combinations as redcurrant jelly with lamb and rowan jelly with venison.

GUIDELINES FOR MAKING JELLIES

Fruits that are high in acid and pectin will make a well-set jelly; others can be combined with another pectin source such as apples or redcurrants. The guidelines for jam (page 122) also apply to jellies, but they have a few extra rules of their own:

1   The fruit must be fresh, but it doesn't need to be peeled or cored. Be sure to remove any blemished specimens, large bits of stem and leaves.
2   Once the fruit has been cooked in the normal way, it needs to be strained. By far the easiest way of doing this is with a jelly bag made of coarse cloth. (This can be purchased from most good shops specialising in kitchen equipment.) Scald the bag in boiling water before use. All kinds of improvised arrangements can be constructed for straining: the bag can be hooked across the legs of an upturned chair, which can be balanced on the edge of a table or rested on a second chair. Place a bowl under the bag to collect the juice from the fruit.
3   Put the fruit pulp into the bag and allow the juice to drip out at its own pace. Don't be tempted to squeeze or agitate the bag as this will make

the juice – and the jelly – cloudy. If the fruit is rich in pectin, you can strain the juice twice: return the pulp to the pan after straining, mix with half the original quantity of water, bring to the boil, then strain again.

4 Measure the volume of juice and for each pint (600 ml) use 1 lb (450 g) white preserving sugar. Sometimes it is possible to use less sugar if the fruit is very rich in pectin.

5 Put the juice in the preserving pan, bring to the boil, then remove from the heat. Stir in the sugar (preferably warmed in the oven). Return to the heat and boil until setting point is reached.

6 Test for setting, pot and cover as for jam.

BLACKCURRANT JELLY

Blackcurrants are very rich in pectin and they make one of the best jellies of all – clear, wine-red in colour and ideal with lamb or mutton. As well as being served on the side of the plate, it can be used as part of a basting sauce for the joint. Simply melt some of the jelly and mix it with orange juice and a little mustard.

A similar jelly can be made from redcurrants or a blend of redcurrants and whitecurrants.

Makes about 2 lb (1 kg)

2 lb (1 kg) blackcurrants	white sugar
1½ pints (900 ml) water	

Pick over the fruit, discarding any rotten or blemished specimens, and wash well. Put into a preserving pan with 1 pint (600 ml) water and simmer gently, mashing well with a wooden spoon during cooking. When the fruit is soft, strain the juice through a jelly bag.

Put the fruit pulp back into the pan with 10 fl oz (300 ml) water and simmer again. Strain and add the juice to the first extract. Measure the total volume and for each pint (600 ml) measure out 1 lb (450 g) white sugar.

Pour the juice into the preserving pan, bring to the boil, then stir in the sugar. Continue boiling fast until setting point is reached. Pour into clean, warmed jars and cover in the usual way.

APPLE JELLY

This is a versatile, all-purpose jelly that goes well with pork and other fatty meats. Use sharp 'Bramley' or other cooking apples if possible.

Makes about 1 lb (450 g)

2 lb (1 kg) apples   white sugar
1 pint (600 ml) water

Wash the apples well, then chop them roughly – there is no need to peel or core them. Put into a preserving pan with the water and simmer until soft, stirring well with a wooden spoon during cooking to prevent the mixture sticking to the bottom of the pan. Strain the pulp through a jelly bag.

Measure the volume of juice and for every 1 pint (600 ml) weigh out 1 lb (450 g) white sugar. Return the juice to the preserving pan, add the sugar and stir well. Bring to the boil and cook rapidly until setting point is reached. Pour into clean, warmed jars and cover in the usual way.

APPLE AND BASIL JELLY

Herb-flavoured jellies can be made by preparing an infusion of the herb and using gelatine and artificial colouring to obtain the correct texture and appearance. But the best way is to use apple (or lemon) jelly as a base and flavour it with the *fresh* herb of your choice. You can experiment with different combinations of herbs and jellies as you wish, but the principle is always the same. For instance, a similar jelly can be made with mint (use 6 fresh leaves) and a sprig of flowering mint put into the jar for decoration. Alternatively, try the same idea with fresh sage.

Makes about 1 lb (450 g)

1 pint (600 ml) Apple Jelly (see   6 sprigs fresh basil
   above)
2 tablespoons (2 × 15 ml spoons)
   lemon juice

Melt the jelly in a preserving pan and add the lemon juice and fresh basil. Bring to the boil and cook until setting point is reached. Remove the sprigs of herbs and pour the jelly into clean, warmed jars. Cover in the usual way.

Alternatively you can start from scratch. Prepare the apple juice as described for Apple Jelly (page 131) and add the lemon juice and basil when you add the sugar. Then proceed in the usual way.

LEMON JELLY

Another very useful jelly with a subtle balance of sharpness and sweetness. It can also be used as a base for herb jellies.

Makes about 1 lb (450 g)

6 lemons   white sugar
1 pint (600 ml) water

Wash the lemons well and chop into pieces. Put into a large bowl, cover with water and leave to stand overnight. Next day transfer to a preserving pan, bring to the boil and cook for 2 hours. Then strain through a jelly bag.

Measure the volume of juice and for every 1 pint (600 ml) weigh out 1 lb (450 g) sugar. Return the juice to the pan, add the sugar and boil until setting point is reached. Pour into clean, warmed jars and cover in the usual way.

LEMON AND MARJORAM JELLY

Lemon jelly can be flavoured with different herbs. The process is very simple, and you can vary the flavourings as you wish – sage and rosemary both work well.

Makes about 1 lb (450 g)

1 pint (600 ml) Lemon Jelly (see   6 sprigs fresh marjoram
    page 132)

Melt the lemon jelly in a preserving pan, add the fresh marjoram and proceed as for Apple and Basil Jelly (page 131).

Alternatively start from scratch. Prepare the lemon juice as described for Lemon Jelly (page 132). Put the juice in a pan with the sugar and marjoram, bring to the boil and cook to setting point. Remove the marjoram and pour the jelly into clean, warmed jars. Cover in the usual way.

ROWAN JELLY

The bright orange berries of the rowan or mountain ash (*Sorbus aucuparia*) are unmistakable on wild heathland trees and on their urban relatives planted neatly by town councils. But you need to be quick if you want to beat the birds to the harvest.

Rowan berries are dry and lack pectin, so you need to add some apples (or wild crabapples) to make a satisfactory jelly. The smoky aroma and slightly bitter taste is perfect with mountain and moorland meat such as grouse and venison; it is also excellent with cold roast pheasant.

Makes about 1 lb (450 g)

1 lb (450 g) rowan berries   1 pint (600 ml) water
8 oz (225 g) apples or crabapples   white sugar

Wash the berries and apples; roughly chop the apples. Put all the fruit into a preserving pan with about 1 pint (600 ml) water – or sufficient to cover the fruit. Simmer until soft, stirring from time to time.

Strain through a jelly bag and measure the volume of juice. For every 1 pint (600 ml) measure out 1 lb (450 g) white sugar. Return the juice to the preserving pan, bring to the boil and add the sugar. Boil vigorously until setting point is reached, then pot and cover in the usual way.

FRUIT BUTTERS AND CHEESES

The pulp remaining after fruit has been strained through a jelly bag can form the basis of fruit butters and cheeses. As their name suggests, fruit butters have a soft, buttery consistency. Because they include less than the normal amount of sugar, they do not keep for long periods, so make them in small batches. They can be spiced and used like jam.

Fruit cheeses are similar to butters, but they are more solid and made with more sugar. They were elegant luxuries in Victorian times and were served as desserts in the grand style at dinner parties. At one end of the table there might be dark damson cheeses, piled high on top of one another and doused in port wine; at the other, elaborate crabapple cheeses studded with hazelnuts and decorated with whirls of whipped cream.

Fruit cheeses keep well; after a year or two in the larder they become encrusted with sugar. They should be potted in straight-sided jars, so that they can be turned out whole and either served as a dessert or sliced and eaten as a kind of 'fruit pâté' with cold pheasant and other game.

PLUM BUTTER

Plum butter is not only an excellent sweet preserve, but it can also be used as the basis for a plum sauce in Chinese cooking – especially with that marvellous ceremonial dish, Peking duck.

A similar butter can be made from damsons instead of plums.

Makes about 3 lb (1.5 kg)

2 lb (1 kg) ripe, dark-skinned plums	about 5 fl oz (150 ml) water white sugar

Wash the plums, slit the skins and put into a pan with the water. Cook slowly. When they are soft, press through a sieve until only the skins and stones are left. Weigh the pulp and for each 1 lb (450 g) measure out 12 oz (350 g) white sugar. Boil the fruit pulp and sugar together in a preserving pan, stir well and continue to cook until the preserve has a thick creamy consistency.

Pot into small, clean jars. If you want to keep the butter for several months, it is a good idea to reinforce the normal cover with an extra seal such as parchment paper. This butter will keep for about 3 months, but it is best used within 1 month.

APPLE BUTTER

This recipe was brought to America by the Pennsylvania Dutch, and it is served as a Thanksgiving dish to commemorate their voyage to the New World in 1734. A similar preserve was made in nineteenth-century England under the name of 'apple marmalade'. In both cases the apples were cooked in cider and mixed with sugar and spices.

Makes about 4 lb (1.75 kg)

2 pints (1.2 litres) sweet cider
4 lb (1.75 kg) ripe apples
1 lb (450 g) soft brown sugar
1 teaspoon (1 × 5 ml spoon)
    ground cloves

2 teaspoons (2 × 5 ml spoons)
    ground cinnamon
½ teaspoon (½ × 5 ml spoon)
    ground allspice

Pour the cider into a preserving pan and boil until it is reduced by half. Peel, core and chop the apples and add to the cider. Cook slowly until the fruit is soft, stirring well to prevent sticking.

Press the apple mixture through a sieve and return the pulp to the pan with the sugar and spices. Simmer until the mixture thickens and has a smooth, creamy consistency. Pour the butter into clean, warmed jars and cover in the usual way.

BLACKBERRY CHEESE

If you are making bramble jelly, why not prepare this fruit cheese at the same time – or vice versa? Like most such cheeses, it is equally versatile as a sweet dessert or as an accompaniment to game.

Makes about 3 lb (1.5 kg)

2 lb (1 kg) blackberries
juice 1 lemon
5 fl oz (150 ml) water

white sugar
a little olive oil

Sort through the blackberries and wash them well, discarding any that are rotten or blemished. Put the fruit into a preserving pan with the lemon juice and water; cook slowly until soft, mashing the fruit and stirring well with a wooden spoon.

Strain the juice through a bag and use to make jelly. Keep the pulp and press through a sieve until only the pips are left. Weigh the pulp and for every 1 lb (450 g) measure out 1 lb (450 g) sugar. Put the pulp and sugar in the preserving pan, bring to the boil and cook until the mixture thickens. It is ready when a spoon drawn across the bottom of the pan leaves a clean line.

Brush warmed straight-sided jars with a little olive oil before filling (this makes it easier to turn out the cheese whole when it is ready to be served). Cover with a waxed disc and seal in the normal way.

MARMALADES

One morning, a ship from Spain, long buffeted by easterly gales, reached Tayside and deposited a cargo of oranges. Among those gathered at the quayside was James Keiller. The oranges were going cheap, and James was tempted to buy a considerable quantity – rashly, as it seemed, for owing to their bitter taste he was unable to sell them. What was to be done? His thrifty and resourceful young wife supplied the answer. We may assume that she was already skilled in the making of jams and jellies; but little could she have dreamed, as she stood over her kitchen fire, boiling and testing, that the result of her experiment would achieve world-wide renown.

(From *The Scots Kitchen* by F. Marian McNeill, Blackie, 1929.)

And that's how citrus marmalade was 'invented'. But the origins of the preserve – and its name – go back to Roman times, when a delicacy called *melimelum* was made from quinces and honey, wine and spices. The Portuguese for quince (*marmelo*) was later transformed into 'marmelade', and preserves going by this name were popular through the Middle Ages and well into the seventeenth century. Orange marmalades appeared around this time but, like their predecessors, they were solid sweetmeats, imprinted with moulds and sprinkled with sugar.

James Keiller's marmalade was different, not only because it was more like a spread, but also because it contained strips of whole peel. Scotland's claim on marmalade was soon challenged by the English, in particular a grocer's wife from Oxford. In 1870 Mrs Cooper started to make marmalade on a small scale, selling it to undergraduates. Like the Keillers over the border, the Coopers soon had to set up a factory to cope with the demand. Stoneware jars and many-sided pots made of fragile china appeared on the breakfast tables of middle-class families throughout the land, and the fashion has lasted.

There is one crucial difference between today's marmalade and its forebears. Most commercial manufacturers – Keillers and Coopers included – now use orange pulp rather than whole fruit as their starting material. It is packed into big tins or drums, sterilised or pumped with sulphur dioxide to preserve it on its journey from Spain to England. But most small manufacturers, cottage industries and people who make their own marmalade at home reckon that the commercially produced versions are usually inferior. There is something about the contrast between the textures of jelly, flesh and peel in a marmalade made from whole fruit that cannot be matched with pulp; connoisseurs also think that pulp can produce murky results, with no intensity of flavour or real character. Make you own and decide for yourself.

GUIDELINES FOR MAKING MARMALADE

1   Fruit

Most marmalade is made from bitter Seville oranges – which are imported not only from Seville, but from Malaga and Sicily as well. Shipments start to arrive in December and continue for about three months, so the best time for marmalade-making is around the end of January, when the fruit is plentiful and before the poorer end-of-season consignments appear.

Other citrus fruit such as lemons and grapefruit can be used at almost any time of the year. Tangerines are not suitable for marmalade unless mixed with other citrus fruit. If you try to bulk out supplies of Sevilles with sweet oranges, you may find that the marmalade is cloudy. Other fruit, such as apricots, can be mixed with citrus fruit to vary the flavours.

Citrus fruit needs to be scrubbed well before you start because the peel is part of the marmalade. Try to obtain *unwaxed* fruit if possible (branches of Safeway now stock unwaxed lemons and oranges).

2   The basic method

(a) Soak the fruit for a couple of minutes in boiling water to make peeling easier. The details of peeling and preparing the fruit vary from recipe to recipe, but there are a few points worth bearing in mind. Chop the peel by hand or use a marmalade cutter; don't mince it as this produces a very pasty result. Remember: the thicker the slices of peel, the longer they will take to cook and soften. Keep the cut peel in a bowl of water until you need it: this prevents it from drying out.

(b) The pectin in citrus fruit is contained mainly in the pith and pips, which are usually put into a muslin bag and removed at the end of the cooking time before the sugar is added.

(c) Cook the fruit in water to soften the peel and extract the pectin. As a very general rule use 2 pints (1.2 litres) water for every 1 lb (450 g) fruit in an open pan. (Halve the amount of water if you are using a closed pressure cooker.) For very large quantities, the amount of water can be reduced. Cooking usually takes about 2 hours in an open pan, depending on the quantity and condition of the fruit. The peel should be soft, so that it disintegrates when squeezed between the fingers.

(d) Warm the sugar before use in a low oven. Remove the preserving pan from the heat and stir in the sugar until dissolved. If you add the sugar too soon, the peel tends to toughen.

(e) Once the sugar has dissolved, boil the marmalade rapidly until setting point is reached. This usually takes 15–20 minutes. Don't overcook as this spoils the colour; also be careful about testing, because the setting point for citrus fruits passes very quickly.

(f) Skim the marmalade, allow it to cool for a few minutes, then pot and cover as for jams (page 125). Stored in a cool, dark place, marmalade will keep for several months.

SEVILLE ORANGE MARMALADE

The classic marmalade, made from bitter Seville oranges. In this recipe there are chunky slices cut from whole peel with pith, as well as orange flesh and pulp. As a variation you can spice the marmalade by adding 2 teaspoons (2 × 5 ml spoons) coriander seeds for each 1 lb (450 g) fruit; these should be put into the muslin bag with the pips. Spirits such as whisky and brandy can also be used to give the marmalade an extra boost: add 1 tablespoon (1 × 15 ml spoon) per 1 lb (450 g) fruit towards the end of the cooking, after the sugar.

Makes about 8 lb (3.5 kg)

3 lb (1.5 kg) Seville oranges
juice 2 lemons

6 pints (3.5 litres) water
6 lb (2.75 kg) white sugar

The skins of the fruit can be quite dirty, so wash them well. Cut the oranges in half, squeeze out the juice and remove the pips. Cut the peel into shreds or strips, chop the flesh and put into a preserving pan with the pips (tied in a muslin bag), lemon juice and water. Simmer for about 2 hours or until the peel is very soft.

Take out the muslin bag and squeeze it well so that any juice goes back into the pan. Remove the pan from the heat and stir in the sugar until it has dissolved. Put the pan back on the stove and boil rapidly until setting point is reached. Let the marmalade stand, away from the heat, for 10 minutes, then give it a final stir to disperse the peel before pouring into clean, warmed jars. Cover and seal in the usual way. Store in a cool place. For best results the marmalade should be kept for a month or two before opening.

DARK COARSE-CUT MARMALADE

A variation on a theme. Brown sugar and molasses provide the 'darkness' for this marmalade; the peel is cut thick and the flesh chopped roughly to give a chunky texture. You can also lace the marmalade with alcohol (see the introduction to Seville Orange Marmalade, page 139).

Makes about 8 lb (3.5 kg)

3 lb (1.5 kg) Seville oranges	6 lb (2.75 kg) soft brown sugar
1 lemon	2 tablespoons (2 × 15 ml spoons)
6 pints (3.5 litres) water	black treacle

Wash the oranges and lemon well, cut in half and squeeze out the juice and pips. Cut the peel into thick strips and chop the flesh roughly. Put the flesh, juice, peel and pips (tied in a muslin bag) into a preserving pan with the water and cook gently for about 2 hours or until the peel has softened and the volume has been reduced by about half.

Remove the pan from the heat, take out the bag of pips and stir in the sugar and treacle. When it has dissolved, boil the marmalade rapidly until setting point is reached. Remove from the heat, allow to cool for a few minutes, then pot and cover in the usual way. This marmalade must be stored for at least 3 months before it is opened. Once aged, it becomes deliciously syrupy and potent.

THREE-FRUIT MARMALADE

Marmalade isn't simply a winter preserve dictated by supplies of Seville oranges. Clare Benson of Clare's Kitchen in Rendcomb, Gloucestershire, produces different kinds throughout the year. This recipe is one for the summer season.

Makes about 10 lb (4.5 kg)

6 lb (2.75 kg) mixed citrus fruit
  (say, 4 sweet oranges, 6
  lemons, 4 grapefruit)

2 pints (1.2 litres) water
6 lb (2.75 kg) white sugar

Wash the fruit well. Mince or chop roughly to the chunkiness you require, discarding any pips. Put into a preserving pan with the water and cook slowly for about 2 hours or until the peel is soft and can be squashed between the fingers. (If you use a pressure cooker, 10 fl oz (300 ml) water will be sufficient and the cooking time can be reduced.)

Remove the pan from the heat and stir in the sugar. Boil for about 20 minutes or until setting point is reached. Allow to cool, stir to disperse the fruit, then pot and cover in the usual way.

APRICOT AND ORANGE MARMALADE

Different fruits can be used to vary the flavours of conventional marmalades. This recipe produces a thick, pulpy preserve rather like a jam.

Makes about 10 lb (4.5 kg)

2 lb (1 kg) Seville oranges
2 lemons
12 oz (350 g) dried apricots

8 pints (4.5 litres) water
8 lb (3.5 kg) sugar

Wash the oranges and lemons and cut them into quarters. Remove the pips and tie in a muslin bag. Pare off the peel and cut into strips. Then chop the flesh of the citrus fruit and the dried apricots and put into a preserving pan. Add the water, peel and muslin bag of pips and leave overnight.

Next day bring the mixture to the boil and simmer for about 2 hours or until the peel is very tender. Remove from the heat, take out the muslin bag and stir in the sugar. Bring to the boil and cook rapidly for about 20 minutes or until setting point is reached. Remove from the heat, allow the marmalade to cool for a few minutes, then pot and cover in the usual way.

FRUIT *IN* SYRUP

It was the Romans who developed the idea of preserving whole fruit in syrup. Although they knew about sugar, they preferred to use honey in the kitchen, and their preserves were packed into wide-necked flagons covered with willow twigs. Sugar was brought to Britain along with spices by soldiers returning from the Crusades, and by the late Middle Ages it had started to make an impression on cooking here. But it was expensive and only the rich could afford to make delicacies such as 'Wardons in syrippe'. (Wardens were large, rock-hard pears ideally suited to this method of preserving.)

As the list of fruit grown in English gardens increased, so did the range of preserves made in the kitchen and, by the middle of the eighteenth century, cooks were using everything from quinces and nectarines to medlars in a mixture of brandy and sugar syrup. Judging by the recipes, many of these items were 'lusciously sweet' and they were prohibitively expensive to make. This is still true, but they are worth producing as occasional treats – especially if you are looking for something unusual to go with meat or game, or need an 'instant' dessert.

GUIDELINES FOR PRESERVING FRUIT
IN SYRUP

1   Choose fruit that is *just* ripe. If it is too soft, it will not preserve well. Because they retain their shape, hard fruit such as plums, pears, apricots and peaches are more successful than strawberries and raspberries.

2   Wipe the fruit with a damp cloth. It may be necessary to prick fruits such as plums with a needle to allow the syrup to penetrate more quickly.

3   After the fruit has been steeped in sugar, it should be packed in clean jars and completely covered with syrup. Other flavourings such as brandy can be added at this stage.

4   The jars should be should be sealed with plastic twist-on caps or corks dipped in wax. Preserving jars with a rubber seal and a metal clasp are also suitable. Once opened, the fruit will not keep for long, so make small batches at a time. For a long shelf-life, sterilise the jars (see page 109).

PRESERVED GREENGAGES

An 'elegant and very rich preserve' made by the basic method without any additional flavourings. Use large, firm greengages and serve as a luscious dessert with whipped cream.

Makes about 1 lb (450 g)

1 lb (450 g) greengages   1 lb (450 g) white sugar

Remove the stalks from the greengages and wipe with a damp cloth. Put into a pan, cover with water and bring to the boil. Remove after 1 minute and lay on a clean cloth to drain. Then peel carefully.

Put the whole fruit into a bowl and strew with sugar. Leave overnight. Next day transfer the fruit and syrupy juice to a preserving pan and simmer for 5 minutes. Repeat this process once a day for 3 successive days until the syrup has thickened and concentrated. Then carefully lift out the greengages and pack them into clean, warmed jars. Boil up the syrup once more, allow to cool, then pour over the fruit, making sure that they are covered. Seal and store until needed.

PRESERVED ORANGES

Use thin-skinned, firm, sweet oranges for this preserve, which sets to a thin jelly once it has cooled. It goes well with potted duck or smoked chicken.

Makes about 3 lb (1.5 kg)

6 oranges
1½ lb (750 g) white sugar   5 fl oz (150 ml) dry white wine

Wipe the orange skins with a damp cloth, then cut into slices less than ¼ inch (5 cm) thick. Do not use the outer slices that contain no flesh, and discard any pips. Arrange the slices carefully in a shallow dish and cover with sugar. Leave overnight.

Next day put the oranges and syrup into a preserving pan, bring to the boil and simmer until the slices feel tender and look transparent. (Add a little water if the syrup looks too thick.) Just before removing from the heat pour in the wine and stir very gently without damaging the slices. Pack the oranges in clean, warmed, wide-mouthed jars, pour over the syrup and cover in the usual way.

PRESERVED PEACHES

A splendid preserve, full of richness and colour. It is excellent served with honey-roast gammon or potted game. The recipe also works well with apricots.

Makes about 2 lb (1 kg)

2 lb (1 kg) medium-sized yellow   1 lb (450 g) white sugar
  peaches   5 fl oz (150 ml) brandy

Wipe the peaches with a damp cloth and plunge into boiling water for 1 minute. Remove and peel carefully. Either leave the fruit whole or cut them in half and discard the stones. Put the peaches into a bowl with the sugar and leave overnight.

Next day transfer the fruit and juice to a preserving pan and simmer gently for about 5 minutes. Do not overcook or the peaches will start to disintegrate. Remove the fruit and pack into clean, warmed jars. Boil up the syrup and add the brandy. Pour over the fruit so that it is completely covered. Seal and store until needed.

OTHER PRESERVES

LEMON CURD

Curds are curious preserves. Like jams they contain fruit and sugar, but they include eggs and butter too. As a result they don't keep indefinitely and should be eaten within 1 month.

Other citrus fruit such as oranges and limes can be made into curds, and the same recipes can be adapted for blackberries with apples and – surprisingly – cooked marrow.

Makes about 1½ lb (750 g)

4 lemons	1 lb (450 g) white sugar
4 oz (100 g) butter	4 eggs, beaten

Grate the rind of the lemons so that only the zest is removed; squeeze the juice from the fruit. Put the rind and juice into the top of a double saucepan with the butter and sugar. (Alternatively use a basin over a saucepan of hot water.) Simmer very slowly and stir until the sugar has dissolved and blended with the butter.

Add the beaten eggs and continue to cook *very* slowly, stirring well, until the mixture starts to thicken and covers the back of a wooden spoon. (If there are signs of curdling, remove from the heat and whisk sharply. Then put back on the stove.)

When the curd is ready, pour into small, warmed jars and cover in the usual way. Store in a cool, dry place and use within 1 month.

RUM BUTTER

The Lake District's most popular souvenir food was once an essential part of every christening feast. During the celebrations there would be plenty of spiced ale, fingers of cheese for unmarried women to tuck under their pillows at night for luck in love, oatcakes and a big bowl of rum butter, which might even be given to the baby 'as its first taste of earthly food'.

These days rum butter is associated with Christmas but not much else. It's worth making your own, and you can substitute brandy for rum if you wish.

Makes about 12 oz (350 g)

8 oz (225 g) unsalted butter
4 oz (100 g) soft brown sugar
3 tablespoons (3 × 15 ml spoons)
    dark rum

squeeze of lemon juice (optional)
pinch of grated nutmeg

Cut the butter into small pieces, put into a warmed bowl and cream with a wooden spoon. (This gives better results than melting the butter.) Add the brown sugar, rum and lemon juice (if using) and mix well using a spoon or your fingers. Add a pinch of grated nutmeg, taste the butter and adjust the flavours if necessary – a little more sweetness, or sharpness, or spice, as you wish.

Pack the butter into a dish and keep in a cool place until needed.

CANDIED PEEL

Candied peel originated in fourteenth-century France when oranges were a luxury of the rich. In those days the peel was boiled, allowed to steep in honey and finally drained and packed in layers sprinkled with powdered ginger.

Many candied fruits and flowers are decorative whimsies, but candied peel has real usefulness. And if you make your own, you can guarantee its quality: much commercial peel, for example, has added sulphur dioxide as a preservative.

Makes about 1 lb (450 g)

4 oranges	8 oz (225 g) white sugar
2 lemons	8 oz (225 g) glucose
1 grapefruit	1 pint (600 ml) water

Wash the fruit well. Remove the peel and cut into tiny cubes or strips. Boil for about 1 hour in a pan of water. Drain thoroughly and put to one side in a bowl.

Make a syrup by mixing together the sugar and glucose with the water. Bring to the boil and pour over the peel. Leave to stand for 2–3 days. Then strain off the syrup, re-boil and pour over the fruit once again. Repeat this process every day until the peel looks transparent and the syrup is very thick.

Remove the peel from the syrup and dry it on a tray in the oven at gas mark ¼, 225°F (110°C). Store the candied peel in bottles away from the light or in boxes between layers of greaseproof paper. It will keep well for many months.

MINCEMEAT

In Elizabethan times mince pies actually contained meat. They were made from a mixture of shredded mutton or beef with suet, plenty of spices, saffron and an assortment of dried fruit including raisins and prunes. By the end of the seventeenth century, cooks had discovered that the rich mixture of suet, spices and fruit would keep well if laced with brandy and stored in stone jars until it was needed, provided that the meat was not added until the pies were ready to be made. From there it was a short step to leaving out the meat altogether, and recipes began to appear for 'mince pies without meat'.

Meatless mincemeat is easy to make and is a fine addition to the larder.

The recipe can be varied – for example you can include apricots or dates, change the spices or add other ingredients such as chopped almonds.

Makes about 3 lb (1.5 kg)

4 oz (100 g) Candied Peel (see page 146)
1 lb (450 g) cooking apples
8 oz (225 g) shredded beef suet
4 oz (100 g) raisins
4 oz (100 g) sultanas
4 oz (100 g) currants
8 oz (225 g) soft brown sugar
1 teaspoon (1 × 5 ml spoon) grated nutmeg
rind and juice 2 oranges
4 tablespoons (4 × 15 ml spoons) brandy

Chop the peel and apples and mix with the suet in a bowl. Add all the other ingredients, stirring well until the mincemeat is thoroughly blended. Pack the mixture closely into clean jars, seal well and store for at least 14 days before using. The mincemeat should keep for 3 months if left unopened.

PARSLEY HONEY

This is actually a herb syrup rather than a true honey. It was made a great deal in country districts during the Second World War when real honey was scarce. It was a good way of using up parsley that had gone to seed, and it provided useful vitamins and other nutrients.

Makes about 2 lb (1 kg)

5 oz (150 g) parsley
1½ pints (900 ml) water
1 lb (450 g) white sugar
juice 1 lemon

Wash the parsley well, discarding any dead leaves, and dry thoroughly. Chop up finely and put into a preserving pan with the water. Boil until the volume is reduced to approximately 1 pint (600 ml). Remove the pan from the heat and stir in the sugar and lemon juice. Return to the heat and boil for about 20 minutes or until the mixture is of a thick, honey-like consistency. Pour into clean, warmed jars and cover while still hot.

CHAPTER ELEVEN

CIDER

Cider has been part of English life for almost a thousand years. It has been drunk by rich and poor; its virtues have been extolled by doctors and physicians; it has served as an item of trade, as wages and as a political weapon; no other drink – not even wine or mead – has been endowed with such magic and power.

The story of cider probably began with the Celts, who plundered little crabapple trees growing in the wild and made a potent liquor from the sour acidic fruit. Later the Anglo-Saxons tended *aeppel-tuns* (orchards) and drank *appeal-win* which was probably a form of rough unsweetened cider. When the Normans set foot on English soil, they brought well-established cider-making skills with them and planted orchards in many parts of the land – from Kent and Sussex, down through Wiltshire and Dorset to the West Country, north into East Anglia, and through Buckinghamshire into Gloucester, Hereford and Worcester.

Cider gained ground through the Middle Ages and Elizabethan times as gardens and orchards improved, but it wasn't until the middle of the seventeenth century that it made a real impact. By that time there were around 350 different varieties of cider apple, and the moment was right for the appearance of cider's first champion, the young Lord Scudamore. By his 'skilful hand' cider became elegant, sophisticated and fashionable. It was drunk from ornate fluted glasses like the best champagne, and Scudamore even devised a way of putting it into bottles as well as casks. This was cider's first golden age, there were arcane treatises and books on the subject and much talk of ingenious processes and equipment for propagating and pressing.

Taxation, agricultural depressions, the coming of industrialisation and new technology all served to change cider's fortunes and character over the years. By the 1960s traditional farmhouse 'scrumpy' was still being made by a few hardline devotees in the West Country, but its image was still rustic, not to say rusty. The large cider-making factories were turning their attention to producing a drink that was appealing, yet completely standardised. Like their colleagues in the brewing industry, they were convinced that 'keg' was the answer. They began to use apple concentrates from all parts of the world as their starting material and they filtered, pasteurised and carbonated their cider; they added preservatives, enzymes, artificial colourings and sweeteners and packed the results in pressurised metal kegs so that it would keep almost indefinitely.

As it turned out, traditional cider was simply waiting for a well-timed revival. In the wake of the highly persuasive and successful efforts of the Campaign for Real Ale (CAMRA), 'real' traditional cider found a new lease of life. But what exactly is 'traditional' cider? CAMRA's cider off-shoot, APPLE, has issued its own set of guidelines. Traditional cider should not be pasteurised; not be filtered; not receive enzyme treatment; not contain preservatives; not have the natural yeast replaced by a cultured yeast; not have a nitrogen source added unless essential to start fermentation; only contain sweeteners if it is labelled 'medium' or 'sweet' and only safe ones to be used; not contain apple concentrate and not contain extraneous carbon dioxide.

Traditional cider now has some new champions: John Chevallier-Guild of Aspall Cyder in Suffolk, who was the first to make commercial cider from organically grown, unsprayed fruit; Julian Temperley, one of the new campaigners in Somerset; and Ivor and Susie Dunkerton in Herefordshire. The Dunkertons have that spirit of pioneering enterprise essential in the 'real food revolution'. They use unsprayed fruit and eschew additives of all kinds; they are also committed to preserving and resurrecting old varieties of cider apple – thus helping to ensure that these special fruit are not bulldozed out of existence. Budding cider-makers should follow their lead by searching out genuine varieties of unsprayed fruit and by taking note of the APPLE nine-point plan.

GUIDELINES FOR MAKING CIDER

At its best, traditional cider is pure fermented juice with nothing added: no sugar, no extra yeast, not even water.

1   Equipment

Producing cider at home needs no special or expensive equipment – in fact the whole process is less complicated than making wine or beer. You need to devise some way of crushing the apples and extracting the juice, but otherwise the process is quite straightforward. Glass flagons or gallon jars, bottles, corks or stoppers, plus fermentation locks and a plastic tube for siphoning are the main requisites. These can be obtained from any home-brew shop or chemist, such as Boots.

All equipment needs to be thoroughly washed and cleaned before you begin; corks need to be boiled in water for 30 minutes before they are used.

2   Apples

The perfect cider apple should have a unique and delicate balance of three elements: sugar, acid and tannin. The sugar produces the alcohol, the acid gives sharpness, and tannin provides a complex blend of roughness, bitterness and astringency. Few cider apples have all these qualities exactly right. In fact each variety has a different composition, but for convenience there are four main categories:

Sweets: These are low in acid and tannin and produce bland soft cider with no great qualities. They are used mainly to tone down the stronger elements from other apples. The most common is the 'Sweet Coppin'; 'Court Royal' was a favourite in the past, but is rare today.

Sharps: These are very high in acid and low in tannin. Some varieties of cooking apple, such as 'Crimson King' and 'Brown's Apple', have similar qualities and are often used in place of true cider sharps.

Bittersharps: These are fairly high in both acid and tannin. Many of the great cider apples of the past – such as 'Foxwhelp' and 'Joeby Crab' – were bittersharps, but they are less versatile than bittersweets. Most cooking apples, such as 'Bramley', are bittersharps. Two legendary cider bittersharps are 'Kingston Black' and 'Stoke Red'.

Bittersweets: These are low in acid and high in tannin and are the classic varieties for West Country cider. They are versatile, can be blended with ease and produce smooth subtle flavours. Because they are well balanced, they can also be used to make decent cider without blending. The best bittersweets are late-ripening varieties such as 'Dabinett', 'Yarlington Mill', 'Tremlett's Bitter' and 'Chisel Jersey'.

3   Choosing the fruit

Ideally cider should be made from genuine cider apples, but in practice most people will have to make do with a mixed bag of unidentified varieties. However, it is worth seeking out organically grown, unsprayed fruit if possible. After all, there is little point in trying to produce traditional additive-free cider if you begin with apples that have been sprayed with all manner of potentially toxic pesticides.

Windfalls from your own garden or from those of friends are acceptable, but you must use the fruit quickly and throw out any that are damaged or blemished as they will affect the quality of the cider. Alternatively, make contact with a reliable local grower, who may be willing to let you have a box or two of decent fruit. As a rough guide, you will obtain 1 gallon (4.5 litres) from 15–20 lb (6.75–9 kg) apples, depending on the way you press the fruit.

If you know the varieties and names of the apples, you can blend them according to their acidity and tannin content to suit your taste; or you can make single-variety ciders, as do Ivor and Susie Dunkerton in Herefordshire. Varieties such as 'Yarlington Mill', 'Kingston Black', 'Chisel Jersey' and 'Brown Snout' can be used on their own to make excellent cider. Wild crabapples are also good. Sharp acidic cooking apples such as 'Bramley' and 'Tom Putt' can be used, but are best blended with some sweet varieties to give a more palatable result. Sweet eating apples such as 'Cox's Orange Pippin', 'Quarrendon', 'James Grieve', 'Charles Ross' and so on are useful only when blended with other sharper acidic varieties.

4   Blending

Blending is a matter for experiment, but you can start off with a mixture of equal parts bittersweet, sharp and sweet apples, and work on from there. If you are aiming for a very dry, tangy cider, use two parts sharp apples along with one part bittersweet and one part sweet. If you prefer a sweeter, smoother cider, reverse the proportions and use two parts sweet apples to one part sharp and one part bittersweet. By juggling with the proportions you can obtain a blend that produces exactly the type of cider you want.

5 Extracting the juice

This is the most strenuous part of cider-making: it is no mean feat to extract the juice from, say, 50 lb (22 kg) hard fruit, so any mechanical assistance you can devise will be an advantage. And if you have to do all the work by hand, see if you can enlist some help to lighten the load.

Chop the apples roughly and pack them in batches into a wooden trough, plastic bin or large ceramic bowl – anything, in fact, that is not made of corrosive metal which will be attacked by the acid in the fruit. Crush the apples by pulverising them with a heavy piece of wood or a mallet until you have a coarse but quite solid pulp. (Domestic mincers and food processors are not much use, as they can handle only very small quantities of fruit at a time.)

6 Pressing

The idea is to obtain as much juice as possible from the pulp, with as little physical effort as possible. Home-brew and wine-making shops often sell small presses which can be used for apple pulp. Alternatively you can apply a little ingenuity and construct a device of your own using wooden blocks, perhaps levered down with a car-jack. Or you can pack the pulp into clean boiled hessian or a nylon sack and pass it through an old-fashioned domestic mangle, making sure that you have a plastic or wooden container beneath to catch the juice. Fold over the end of the sack so that no pulp leaks out during pressing. You may need to make two extractions to get all the juice out. Although this method is quite convenient, it is a fast process; for best results pressing should be slow and sustained, so that the juice drips out at its own pace.

7 Fermentation

Apple juice will ferment quite naturally with its own yeast, so it shouldn't be necessary to add cultured yeast to stimulate the process. Transfer the apple juice to a large fermenting bin or white plastic dustbin, depending on the amount you have. Cover the bin closely and put in a warm dark place at 60–70°F (15–21°C) so that fermentation can begin. This happens spontaneously – and often quite violently – for a few days. Keep a close watch on the brew and remove any scum as it forms. When the activity begins to subside and the first fermentation is complete, transfer the cider to 1 gallon (4.5 litre) glass jars (suitably cleaned) and fit each with a cork and a fermentation lock so that carbon dioxide can escape but no air can get in. The cider will continue to ferment, quite quickly at first, but later at a more leisurely pace as the remaining sugars are converted to alcohol. Keep the jars in a warm dark place during this time.

8   Bottling, storing and maturing

After a few weeks, depending on the conditions and the temperature of the cider, fermentation will be almost complete, with only the occasional bubble rising from the jars. You can then remove the fermentation locks, fit the jars with boiled corks and store them in a cool dark place for at least 2–3 months.

Alternatively, you can transfer the cider to pint (600 ml) or quart (1.2 litre) bottles if that is more convenient. Use heavy-duty beer or cider bottles if possible: most wine bottles are not strong enough to withstand the internal pressure that may occur as fermentation is finished. Siphon the cider into cleaned bottles and fill them up to the neck. If you want to create a little extra sparkle or sweetness, add 1 teaspoon (1 × 5 ml spoon) sugar to each pint (600 ml) when bottling. The bottles can be stopped with corks, metal crown tops (in which case a special crimping tool needs to be used), plastic snap closures or old screw tops with unperished rubber rings.

Natural fermentation, the high pectin content of the apples, plus the fact that the cider has not been filtered, mean that it will remain slightly cloudy, even after it has been stored for a few months.

Once you have opened a flagon or bottle, the cider needs to be drunk within 24–48 hours, but that is seldom a problem. Wine locks and vacuum stoppers can be used as a temporary measure.

INDEX

Acid-Curd 'Lactic' Cheese, 30
Acton, Eliza, 113
Apple:
  and Basil Jelly, 131–2
  Butter, 135
  Cider, 149–54
  Jelly, 131
  Pork and Sage Sausage, 53
APPLE, 150
Apricot:
  and Almond Jam, 127–8
  and Orange Marmalade, 141–2
  Vinegar, 117
Ayrton, Elizabeth, 83

Bacon, 33
Bacon, Francis, 9
Bara Brith, 22
Batalia Pye, 82
Bath Chaps, 42
Bear Hotel, Devizes, 92
Beef:
  and Egg Pie, 89
  Pickled, 43
  Potted, 72
  Spiced, 37–8

Stew and Hard, 65–6
  and Tomato Sausage, 55
Benson, Clare, 127, 141
Blackberry Cheese, 136
Blackberry Vinegar, 118
Blackcurrant Jelly, 130
Borrow, George, 69
Botulism, 34
Brawn, 61–2
Bread and Baking, 11–23
  Baking, 15
  Bara Brith, 22
  Doris Grant Loaf, 16
  Flour, 13
  Kneading, 14
  Oatmeal Bread, 17
  Onion Bread, 19–20
  Pitta Bread, 21
  Proving, 14
  Rising, 14
  Shaping, 14
  Soda Bread, 18
  Walnut Bread, 19
  Wholemeal, 100 per cent, 15
  Yeast, 13–14
Brining, 32–4, 36, 99

Brothwell, D. & O., 32
Burdett, Osbert, 25
Butter:
  Apple, 135
  Clarified, 71
  Plum, 134–5
  Rum, 146
Butterworth, Jean, 74

Caerphilly Cheese, 24
Campaign for Real Ale (CAMRA), 150
Candied Peel, 146–7
Caul fat, 62
Char, Potted, 80–1
Cheddar Cheese, 24
Cheeses, Soft, 24–31
  Acid-Curd 'Lactic' Cheese, 30
  Cottage Cheese, 29–30
  Cream Cheese, 31
  Equipment for making, 26–7
  Flavourings, 29
  Guidelines for making, 26–9
  Herb-flavoured, 25
  Milk for, 27
  Rennet for, 26, 27–8
  Starter, 28–9
  Storage, 29
  Unpasteurised, 25
Cheshire Cheese, 24
Chestnut Preserve, 128
  see also Water Chestnuts
Chevallier, John, 150
Chilli Oil, 115–16
Chorleywood Bread Process, 12
Cider, 149–54
  Apples, 151–2
  Blending, 152–3
  Bottling, storing and maturing, 154
  Choosing the fruit, 152
  Equipment, 151
  Extracting the juice, 153
  Fermentation, 153–4

Pressing, 153
Cobbett, William, 33, 38
Colwick Cheese, 25
Combers, Captain Charles, 108
Cooked Meat Products, 59–68
  Brawn, 61–2
  Faggots, 62–4
  Guidelines for preparing, 60–1
  Haslet, 64–5
  Jellied stock for, 61
  Jellied Tongue, 68
  Pork Cheese, 66–7
  Pressed Spice Pork, 67
  Stew and Hard, 65–6
Cooper, Mrs, 137
Cornish Pasties, 93–4
Cottage Cheese, 29–30
Crab, Potted, 79–80
Cream Cheese, 31
Crowdie Cheese, 25
Crumpets, 23
Cumberland Pie, 91
Cumberland Sausage, 54–5

Damson Butter, 134–5
David, Elizabeth, 39, 119
Devizes Pie, 92
Dixon, Peter, 74, 75
Doris Grant Loaf, 16
Double Gloucester Cheese, 24
Doves Farm, 13, 15
Dressings, Salad, 118–20
  Green Herb, 119–20
Dry-salting, 32–5, 99
Duck, Salt, 39
Duck Liver, Potted, with Water
    Chestnuts, 75
Dunkerton, Ivor and Susie, 150, 152

Egg and Beef Pie, 89
Elderberry Ketchup, 113
Evans, Carole and John, 53, 56

Evelyn John, 119

Faggots, 62–3
  Welsh, 63–8
Fish:
  Quin's Fish Sauce, 112
  Smoked, 96–106
Flavoured Oils, 115–16
  Chilli, 115–16
  Garlic and Ginger, 115
  Herb, 116
Flavoured Vinegars, 116–18
  Apricot, 117
  Blackberry, 118
  Rosemary, 117
Flour, 13
  Organic, 13, 15
  Stone-ground, 13
Forfar Bridies, 95
Fruit Butters and Cheeses, 134–6
  Apple Butter, 135
  BLackberry Cheese, 136
  Plum Butter, 134–5
Fruit in Syrup, 142–5
  Guidelines for Preserving, 143
  Preserved Greengages, 143
  Preserved Oranges, 144
  Preserved Peaches, 144–5
Fuller, Thomas, 11

Game Pie, 88
Garlic and Ginger Oil, 115
Gear, Jackie, 16
Ginger and Garlic Oil, 115
Ginger and Rhubarb Jam, 125
Glasse, Hannah, 52, 70, 112
Gloucester Pie, 82
Gooseberry and Orange Jam, 127
Greengages, Preserved, 143
Grigson, Jane, 34, 51

Haggis, 58

Ham, 33
  Potted, with Rosemary, 74
Hartley, Dorothy, 70
Harvey's Sauce, 108
Haslet, 64–5
Herbs:
  Green Herb Dressing, 119–20
  Herb Oil, 116
Horner's Cheese, 25

Jams, 121–8
  Apricot and Almond, 127–8
  Basic method, 124–5
  Chestnut Preserve, 128
  Equipment, 123
  Gooseberry and Orange Jam, 127
  Guidelines for making, 122–5
  Morello Cherry and Walnut Jam,
    126–7
  Pectin, 122–3
  Raspberry Jam, 126
  Rhubarb and Ginger Jam, 125
  see also Jellies; Marmalades
Jellied Tongue, 68
Jellies, 129–33
  Apple Jelly, 131
  Apple and Basil Jelly, 131–2
  Blackcurrant Jelly, 130
  Guidelines for making, 129–30
  Lemon Jelly, 132
  Lemon and Marjoram Jelly, 132–3
  Rowan Jelly, 133
Johnson, Alison and Andrew, 17

Keiller, James, 137
Ketchups and Sauce, 107–14
  Bottling, 109–10
  Elderberry Ketchup, 113
  Guidelines for making, 109–10
  Mushroom Ketchup, 111
  Quin's Fish Sauce, 112
  Oxford Brawn Sauce, 120

Sterilising the bottles, 109
Storing, 110
Tomato Ketchup, 110
Worcestershire Sauce, 108, 114
Kippers, 103–4
Kitchiner, Dr William, 119

Lamb:
  and Mint Sausage, 56
  Salt, 38
Larder, storing in the, 10
Leicester Cheese, 24
Lemon:
  Curd, 145
  Jelly, 132
  and Marjoram Jelly, 132–3
Listeriosis (*Listeria monocytogenes*), 25

MacIver, Mrs, 58
McNeill, F. Marian, 137
Marmalade, 137–42
  Apricot and Orange, 141–2
  Dark Coarse-cut, 140
  Guidelines for making, 138–9
  Seville Orange, 139–40
  Three-fruit, 141
Marriage, Claire and Michael, 15
May, Robert, 59
Meat, Salted and Pickled, 32–45
  Bath Chaps, 42
  Dry-salting, 35
  Equipment, 35
  Ingredients, 34–5
  Pickled Beef, 43
  Pickled Ox Tongue, 44–5
  Pickled Pork, 39–41
  Pickling in brine, 36
  Preparing to cook pickled meat,
    36–7
  Salt Duck, 39
  Salt Mutton/Lamb, 38
  Spiced Beef, 37–8

  see also Cooked Meat Products
Melton Mowbray Pork Pie, 86–7
Miller Howe Hotel, Windermere,
  116
Mincemeat, 147–8
Morello Cherry and Walnut Jam,
  126–7
Muffett, Thomas, 43
Mushroom Ketchup, 111
Mutton:
  Pies, 90
  Salt, 38

Nixon, Bronwen, 81

Oatcakes, 20, 65
Oatmeal Bread/Rolls, 17
Oil *see* Flavoured Oils
Onion Bread, 19–20
Orange(s):
  and Gooseberry Jam, 127
  Marmalade, 137–42
  Preserved, 144
Ox Tongue, Pickled, 44–5
Oxford Brawn Sauce, 120
Oxford Sausage, 52

Parsley Honey, 148
Pasties:
  Cornish, 93–4
  Venison, 94–5
Pastry, 85–6
  Hot-water, 85
  Raising, 86
  Shortcrust, 85
  see also Raised Pies and Pasties
Peaches, Preserved, 144–5
Pectin, 122–3
Pepys, Samuel, 113
Pickled Meat *see* Meat
Pies *see* Raised Pies
Pigeon, Potted, 76

Pigs' Trotters, Pickled, 41
Pistachio Nuts with Pork Sausage, 54
Pitta Bread, 21
Plum Butter, 134–5
Pontac's Sauce, 107, 113
Pork:
Apple and Sage Sausage, 53
Brawn, 61–2
Cheese, 66–7
Cumberland Sausage, 54–5
Faggots, 62–4
Haslet, 64–5
Jellied Tongue, 68
Melton Mowbray Pork Pie, 86–7
Potted, 73
Pressed Spiced, 67
Sausage, 52–3
Sausage with Pistachio Nuts, 54
Toulouse Sausage, 57
Pork, Pickled, 39–41
'Barrelled', 33
Bath Chaps, 42
Belly, 40
Ears and Tails, 41
Hand of, 40
Leg of, 41
Trotters, 41
Potting, Potted, 69–81
Beef, 72
Char, 80–1
Clarified Butter, 71
Crab, 79–80
Duck Liver with Water Chestnuts, 75
Guidelines for, 70–2
Ham with Rosemary, 74
Ingredients, 70
Pigeon, 76
Pork, 73
Potting, 71
Preparations, 71
Seasonings, 71

Shrimps, 78–9
Storing, 72
Venison, 77
Preserves, 121–48
Candied Peel, 146–7
Fruit Butters and Cheeses, 134–6
Fruit in Syrup, 142–5
Jams, 121–8
Jellies, 129–33
Lemon Curd, 145
Marmalades, 137–42
Mincemeat, 147–8
Parsley Honey, 148
Rum Butter, 146

Quin's Fish Sauce, 112

Raffald, Elizabeth, 80
Raised Pies and Pasties, 82–95
Beef and Egg Pie, 89
Cornish Pasties, 93–4
Cumberland Pie, 91
Devizes Pie, 92
Filling, 84
Forfar Bridies, 95
Game Pie, 88
Guidelines for making, 84–6
Jellied stock, 84
Melton Mowbray Pork Pie, 86–7
Mutton Pies, 90
Pastry, 84–5
Venison Pasties, 94–5
Raspberry Jam, 126
Rennet, 26, 27–8
Rhubarb and Ginger Jam, 125
Robinson of Runcorn, Mr, 78–9
Roebuck, Brimfield, 53, 56
Rolls, Oatmeal, 17
Rosemary with Potted Ham, 75
Rosemary Vinegar, 117
Rothay Manor, Ambleside, 81
Rowan Jelly, 133

Rum Butter, 146

Salmon, Smoked, 104–5
Salted and Pickled Meat *see* Meat
Sandys, Lord, 114
Sauces *see* Ketchups and Sauces;
    Dressings
Sausages, 46–58
  Basic filling method, 50–1
  Beef and Tomato, 55
  Chopping and mincing, 48
  Cumberland, 54–5
  Equipment, 48
  Filling, 48–9
  Frozen, 51
  Guidelines for making, 48–51
  Haggis, 58
  Hygiene, 48–9
  Lamb and Mint, 56
  Oxford, 52
  Pork, 52–3
  Pork, Apple and Sage, 53
  Pork, with Pistachio Nuts, 54
  Skin, 49–50
  Storing, 51
  Toulouse, 57
  Venison, 56–7
Scarista House Hotel, Isle of Harris,
    17
Scudamore, Lord, 149
Shrimps, Potted, 78–9
'Slipcote' Cheese, 25
Smoked Fish, 96–106
  Cold- and hot-smoking, 100
  Cooling, 101
  Drying, 99
  Equipment, 98
  Guidelines for smoking, 97–101
  Kippers, 103–4
  Preparing the fish, 98
  Salting and brining, 99
  Smoked Salmon, 104–5

Smoked Sprats, 101–3
Smoked Trout, 105–6
Smoking process, 100–1
Storing, 101
Wood and Smoke, 99–100
Soda Bread, 18
Spiced Beef, 37–8
Sprats, Smoked, 101–3
Stew and Hard, 65–6
Stock, jellied, 84

Temperley, Julian, 150
Tomato and Beef Sausage, 55
Tomato ketchup, 108, 110
Tongue, Jellied, 68
Torry kiln, Aberdeen, 96–7
Toulouse Sausage, 57
Tovey, John, 116
Trout, Smoked, 105–6
Tusser, Thomas, 33

Venison:
  Pasties, 94–5
  Potted, 77
  Sausage, 56–7
Victoria Cheese, 25
Vinegar *see* Flavoured Vinegars

Walnut Bread, 19
Walnut and Morello Cherry Jam,
    126–7
Water Chestnuts with Potted Duck
    Liver, 75
Wensleydale Cheese, 24
White, Florence, 92, 108
White, Gilbert, 111
White Moss House, Grasmere, 74, 75
Wholemeal Bread, 100 per cent, 15
Woodger, John, 103
Worcestershire Sauce, 108, 114

Yeast, 13–14